A Gift

from

FRIENDS
OF THE
Palo Alto
LIBRARY

Small by *Design*
Gardens for Any Space

Most people today only have a small backyard or garden, or even a courtyard or balcony, rather than the quarter-acre block of times past. This is the first completely Australian book genuinely focused on small garden design—and design is so important where space is at a premium. As well as detailing design principles, various garden styles are explored, including international styles such as Japanese, Balinese and French provincial, and formal and informal styles. There's information about choosing garden flooring, walls and lighting and putting in the finishing touches. Plants are suggested for various locations. Numerous garden case studies are included, each with an indication of the difficulty of creating such a garden, and a look at the design principles employed and the problems that needed to be overcome.

Beautifully illustrated with photographs by well-known Australian garden photographer Lorna Rose, all of small Australian gardens, the book will be invaluable to landscape architects, town planners, councils, horticulturalists and gardeners of all sorts.

Paul Urquhart has been a gardener since the age of five. He is a garden writer and has been editor of several Australian magazines, currently *Australian House and Garden* and *The (Sydney) Magazine*, published by *The Sydney Morning Herald*. He is the author of several books, including the enormously successful *The New Native Garden*.

Lorna Rose was born in the United Kingdom and became a freelance garden photographer after studying horticulture in Sydney. She shoots anything that grows, but particularly enjoys well-designed gardens, combined with beautiful, appropriate and healthy plants. Her work has appeared in numerous books, magazines and calendars etc.

Small by Design

Gardens for Any Space

Paul Urquhart

Photographs by
Lorna Rose

Contents

Introduction

Gardeners often ask me to recommend a book on small gardens that is geared to Australian conditions, focuses on gardens like those we are used to and uses plants that thrive in our climates. Sadly, there has been little available, particularly with Australian content.

Hence *Small by Design*. This book presents the work of many garden designers, landscape architects and home gardeners, and all the gardens are Australian.

Why Small Gardens?

Australia has actually had a small garden tradition since 1788. Apart from on large estates—developed first in the cities and later, in rural districts, by squatters—most houses were small, with small cottage gardens for storing firewood and other household needs in a world before the advent of electricity and other things we take for granted.

Historically, we borrowed the terrace backyard from the English. Even well into the twentieth century, terrace or semi-detached housing was the norm and back gardens were tiny, cramped and used only for storage and to grow food. After World War I there was a drift away from the smoky cities as fresh new garden suburbs sprang up on city fringes, and the quarter-acre block tradition was born.

The concept of outdoor living came from the Americans, particularly the Californians. Ironically, while we share a similar climate with Californians, our garden design has been stuck in a cold-climate rut for too long. A gentle northern climate with plentiful, soft rain and moist air—not too cold, not too hot—is a good recipe for easy gardening, but is it our reality? Unless you live in Mt Macedon (Victoria), or Robertson (New South Wales), it is a world apart from most people's experience. Our gardens are drier, hotter and, well…just different. We celebrate these differences in this book.

In a land-poor world, the wheel has turned full circle. Young people are moving back into the inner cities that their parents or grandparents left nearly a century ago, and rediscovering the small inner-city garden. Population pressure on land has meant that new townhouse and villa-style developments pack more dwellings onto a piece of land, each with a small, or even tiny, garden. Conversely, our wish to build bigger and better houses, disparagingly termed 'McMansions', and the modern trend to renovate and extend, means houses often take up a larger footprint on the land, leaving a smaller garden.

Our small gardens now also have to serve roles similar to those that drove Eastern design. The garden is increasingly seen as a sanctuary. The sterile suburban prairie of a vast lawn dotted with ramshackle sheds and a Hills Hoist is a dying relic, even in older outer suburbs. It is the creation of beauty, and the intangible qualities like serenity, calm and sensuality, that enable us to recharge our emotional batteries after a busy working week. We need our gardens more than ever. They often serve as the only connection with sanity in a weird but wonderful world.

Planning
Spaces

Small gardens demand careful planning to use space efficiently and maximise the perception of space. This is essential in any small space, whether it is a garden or a room inside the house.

Gardens are composed of open spaces—areas of lawn, a body of water or an area of hard surfacing—planted areas and also structures. Together they define the shape and appearance of all spaces. Design needs to be carefully planned to manipulate the interactions between flooring, walling and other hard surfaces with the planted elements of a garden.

Landscape professionals—architects and designers—use tools, often referred to as 'design principles' to manipulate space. These are the tricks of the trade, the gardener's illusions. Used well, they can make the difference between a great small garden and an ordinary garden.

Design Principles

Design is essentially problem solving. In garden design we face both aesthetic issues—such as how to make a space seem larger, an unattractive view look better or decide what is the best way to plant to avoid future problems—and practical issues such as drainage, erosion, shade and warmth. Design principles solve the practical problems and provide solutions that can be both physically attractive and charismatic.

Design principles are simply tried and true ground rules that gardeners have used through the ages to add unity, a soul and long-lasting appeal. They have been finely honed through years of practice and observation. Design principles include: unity, repetition, transition, focalisation, rhythm, balance and proportion/scale. Each principle is dependent on the others to some extent, but all are essential to developing a satisfying design.

These are not solely tools of garden designers. Some come from art. The garden designer's understanding of colour and line are derived from the art world. Designers manipulate levels, focal points, views and materials to create texture and pattern. They create illusions, instil a sense of mystery and surprise and manipulate our perception in order to make a small space seem larger or to create enduring impact when the garden is viewed.

A skilful designer will use these tools to address different conditions, climates, terrains and themes. Used effectively they make small spaces appear larger, narrow spaces seem wider and blot out or disguise unpleasant views.

Following are brief descriptions of some of the important design elements. They will help you interpret design jargon, understand the basic concepts, and see how they can be used to make a great garden. Each principle is dependent on the others to some extent, but all are essential to developing a satisfying design.

Unity

*I*n designing a garden, aim to create unity, a design with a single purpose. Unity is achieved when all the individual elements form a coherent theme, and this often involves employing a unifying element, such as a row of hedging or a repeated motif, using either hard landscaping or soft (plant) material.

Unity comes from setting a design goal and single-mindedly pursuing it. Maintaining consistency between the hard landscape components and planting themes creates harmony. Every element you select should complement the central scheme and serve a functional purpose, whether it is to do with vegetation or buildings. The related notion of balance, on the other hand, compares two segments of a landscape, with each judged separately for their relative weight within the garden (see page 24).

Making a Good Fit

In small spaces, we tend to focus inwards and forget that gardens exist in a broader landscape. The result is a discrete space that may look out of place in the larger context. This introspective way of dealing with unity overlooks another point of view, that of looking out into the wider landscape.

Keeping your garden in sympathy with its surroundings involves accepting limits on what you can or should plant. It does not mean you have to blindly copy neighbours' mistakes, but maintaining the character of your surroundings can enhance a broader sense of unity.

Achieving Unity

Mass planting and repetition are the simplest ways to create unity. Repetition creates unity by repeating similar elements like plants, plant groups or a decorative style throughout the landscape. Hedges, for instance, create a central theme to tie disparate or untidy plantings together. It's like drawing a dark outline around an illustration to make it stand out on the page.

The idea of following a consistent theme is central to create garden unity and harmony. Decorative elements selected on thematic criteria can also individualise and personalise your garden, so avoiding the blandness of copying the neighbours.

This unified combination of colours that are both complimentary and contrasting suggests Middle Eastern elements fused with more contemporary design.

Right: The Mosaic Garden is a Melbourne garden icon. Though the patterns and colours vary, the unity comes from a continuous theme of mosaic applied to all masonry surfaces in a small space.

Below: A fence-covering mass of Burmese honeysuckle unites a disparate planting of subtropical plants with traditional European motifs such as the pebble mosaic pathway and box hedging.

Repetition

Repetition can unify and link the various parts of a garden. You can repeat particular plants, shapes (such as conical or rounded), colours (for example flower or foliage colour), lines, materials or textures as well as architectural features, ornamentation and design themes. Successful repetition creates rhythm, focus, emphasis and unity.

The simplest and most blatant use of repetition is seen in formal gardens, where plants are arranged in rows or along definite axes. In an informal garden, repetition is often more subtle. Strolling through a garden, you may come across a plant or an element that you remember seeing earlier on your walk. The memory of things seen engenders a sense of unity if the design is well executed. However, blanket repetition can be monotonous, for example when too many red- or yellow-leafed plants, clipped box, conifers, dark foliage or small specimens in a large space are used. This is overuse rather than repetition.

Be selective about what you choose to repeat. In an informal landscape, especially a small one, you may only need to repeat one or two plants and perhaps a colour or shape to balance the overall effect.

Unity and simplicity often go hand in hand. Too much variety in a small space creates confusion. Repetition helps remove elements that cause a garden to look 'busy' or cluttered.

The Balance Nexus

Repetition has a natural affinity with balance. Repeating a theme balances a plant composition or grouping in another part of the garden. For example, you might repeat a border in more than one section of the garden. This is the main principle in structured and formal gardens. In naturalistic gardens, repeating the pattern of a group of plants, such as those with a rounded shape, or with large, textured leaves or with silvery foliage.

A rounded ball of box may be balanced by a similar shape, perhaps more oval or concave, using the same plant or another, say a lillypilly, or even the viny muehlenbeckia grown as a mound. Juxtaposing completely different shapes can also create balance. You could also introduce colour contrast, for example the silvery or lime green leaves of aniseed plant (*Helichrysum petiolare*), trained to shape. Similarly, a strappy-leafed silvery *Astelia* could balance perfectly with a purple-leafed form of *Phormium tenax* in another part of the garden. How you blend plants will depend on what else is used in the garden.

Top: Box hedges are here given an edge by creating rounded bosses atop what could have been an ordinary line of hedging.

Bottom left: Repeating the theme of clipped box in the two square pots marking a path serves to maintain unity while also adding a hint of variety. The softening elements, like the billowing seaside daisy, are also repeated. Smart, precise seasonal impatiens give the garden a sense of class.

Bottom right: For a touch of retro appeal on this rooftop garden, galvanised pots filled with *Agave attenuata* were simply lined up along a ledge.

Transition:
Shifting Stages Smoothly

Transition is essentially gradual change. Our gardens are full of changes and the key to designing successfully is to make changes appear measured.

Transition applies to many things, including plant size, texture, hard landscaping, plant height or colour and structural elements. We talk of the internal/external transition from the house to the patio and garden, of the transition from large leaves to small and of texture from rough to smooth. The more seamless these changes, the more successful they will be. Abrupt or sudden changes can be jarring.

In practice, using an intermediate stage between two of the above elements can make for a smooth transition. For example, transition is successful where plants are staggered in size from large to medium trees, to shrubs and groundcovers. To make a seamless change from grass to pavers, you could use stepping stones with grass or mini-mondo growing between.

Using Transition To Create 'Illusion'

Transition is a helpful tool to alter perception and create the illusion of depth in a small garden. To make the garden seem larger than it really is, place taller plants in the foreground and smaller ones beyond, thus creating a visual shift from taller to shorter plants. It changes the perception of depth and distance as an artist uses perspective in a painting. Conversely, starting with shorter plants and moving outwards towards taller plants can frame a focal point, making it stand out and seem closer than it really is.

The transition from outside to inside is much easier on a level surface than on a slope or where the main living spaces are on the first level. Here, ziggurat-like steps wrap around the building and find an echo in the repeated square stepping stones in the lawn.

Slopes	
A downhill slope away from the house makes a space appear larger. Upward slopes gravitating away from the house make the space seem smaller because the view is foreshortened. The latter situation is common on new housing sites in hilly areas. A large, level terrace close to the house will	balance the upper slope. If the area is steep, retaining walls are the best bet. The best placement for an artificial slope on a level site is in the middle distance. It could take the form of a slight rise formed by railway sleepers or a mound of soil planted or terraced and paved.

Glass walls and doors which fold right back are an ideal way to make a seamless transition to the outside. It is the key to how most contemporary buildings interact with the outside. This is a modern addition to a standard Federation semi-detached house.

Changes of Level

Transition can involve changes of level even in a small garden. For example, steps down or up from wide terraces to paths help make a space more visually exciting. A sloping garden provides more opportunity to create this visual interest than a level one, but can be more costly to exploit. Levelling and cut-and-fill operations on steep slopes may involve expensive engineering, wall-building or cantilevered decks.

Raised beds, steps, bridges, boardwalks, cascades and water features often involve level changes. They can use the natural slope or be built into level sites to make them appear less flat.

Transition on a steeply sloping site is made easier by the wide steps and dense planting of the garden, aided by significant plants grown in pots. Another seating platform—a sunny one—is located at the top of the stairs.

Focal Points and Focalisation:
The Attention Grabbers

Focal points in a garden are simply those standout elements that draw the eye and focus attention on a particular spot. We use them to avoid the problem of trying to take in everything in one glance. A focal point can be a specimen plant or group of plants, a structure such as a gazebo, sculpture or water feature, or an entrancing view.

A focal point attracts our attention. Once our attention is grabbed, we are generally drawn towards it and then also to the surrounding garden. Therefore, focal points need careful placement. Focal points can also draw attention away from undesirable elements. Placed in a finished setting, the object should be of high quality and pleasing to the eye.

The act of drawing the eye is called 'focalisation'. Straight lines are more direct and draw attention quicker than curved ones. In a small garden, flowing lines are preferable, as the impact is more measured and therefore effective if attention is drawn slowly.

Symmetrical designs intensify the focalisation, while asymmetrical designs soften or even avoid focalisation. Focalisation is achieved most easily by placing an attractive focal point on an uncluttered lawn or area of paving so there's nothing to compete with it.

There are two ways to use focal points:

- Place a focal point along a main axis or at the end of a garden where you see it from the viewing start point. For example, you might enter the garden from the back door or patio and be attracted to an object at the far end.
- Place a focal point along a path or passageway. It may either draw you towards it, such as would occur with a small seat in a clearing, or it may stop you in your tracks to simply look and take in the surrounding planting.

By slowing us down or directing attention to something other than the main view, focal points change our perceptions; we linger in the garden and it seems bigger and fuller than at first glance.

Opposite: In the face of such a massive external focal point as Sydney's Harbour Bridge, the owners of this harbourside balcony garden chose a beautiful bonsai juniper to redirect attention inward to their apartment's outdoor space.

Below: A simple carved stone water bowl attracts attention along a timber deck. The shape is innately pleasing but the addition of water and established plantings make it 'fit' its position perfectly.

Rhythm and Movement

Sweeping steps up the side of a narrow garden direct us into the open space at the rear of the property. A decorative broom becomes both a metaphor and a focal point as viewers are swept upward. It also slows us down, as the rise requires focusing on the steps.

Spaces can be static or they can convey the impression of movement. In a small garden, linking design elements such as transition, line and pattern gives the perception that there is a flow from one area to another.

There are two main ways of creating movement in small gardens. You can use a main walkway with a terminal focus or feature; or you can create a strong central space, such as those found in many townhouses and terrace houses—the 'outdoor room' concept. In the latter you can use interlocking and overlapping patterns to create a sense of movement. Using line and space, we can slow or speed up passage through a garden.

Levels

Changes of level can create a sense of movement even if no actual walking is involved. On a flat surface, introducing different levels, such as two large intersecting terraces accessed by a single step, can create a sense of movement. Without terracing, a single-level ground space may appear static, even lifeless. The angle at which the terraces interact can also have an impact. Line can be as important here as the actual change of level. A wide, snaking intersection could be less abrupt and more sensual than a more geometric or rectangular intersection.

Linking Spaces

The way spaces are linked and the transitions between them have a profound effect on our perception of movement. We link spaces by means of paths, lawns and steps. Each can unite the spatial elements of a garden such as terraces, lawns and patios. Steps link spaces on sloping ground while the straightness of a path can have an immense impact on how quickly we try to reach a destination.

Form Ruled by Function

Function often determines the speed of movement between spaces in a garden. Hanging the washing, going for an early morning dip or refuelling the worm farm are not generally activities we want to dawdle over. We want to take the most direct route. Landscape architects call this tendency the 'desire line'.

Design can control how fast we move through a garden. This in turn has an impact on how large we perceive that space to be. If we move through the garden fast it appears smaller. In a small space, the aim is usually to slow passage, creating a sense of restfulness for us to enjoy. Varying the route achieves this.

A serpentine or curving path slows us down, as does a tree or large container at the end of a path that deviates our route. If we are deliberately slowed down in this way, it's important that there is an object to view or a place to sit and look out at the end.

Tight curves and path width also modulate speed. Narrowing the path makes us speed up, especially if walking with others; wide paths suggest passive enjoyment and slow movement. A slight curve is traversed much quicker than a tight one, making the garden appear smaller.

Creating openings and exits into different parts of a garden also slows passage, often simply by forcing a decision as to which to take. Steps and sloping ground involve changes of level, which also slow us down.

For this display garden, designer Peter Blachak used the shape and form of a barcode to design a wall that mixes widths to give a sense of movement, depending on which side it is viewed from. The rhythm of the alternating narrow and wide gaps creates an illusion of depth.

Mystery and Surprise

Mystery and surprise make a garden interesting. Anything that creates a barrier to seeing the garden in one go can create mystery and surprise. When you look into a garden, if you see it all in one glance there is nothing to encourage you to want to stay. What you see is what you get.

Larger gardens have more opportunity to include nooks and crannies, secret corners that give you a lift when you come across them for the first time.

One way to add surprise to a small garden is to use a device known as 'tension'. Creating enclosed areas within a garden—'garden rooms'—is the most common method. Walls, hedges, lattice and foliage screens can separate sections. See-through screens such as lattice, or certain plants can hide the full view of the garden. Because they allow glimpses of a view, they hint at something beyond the screen. This is because the eye perceives a partial barrier as a real barrier and you tend to focus attention on the foreground rather than what lies beyond, until you venture further to discover what lies there.

The separations provided by devices such as hedges, garden seats, container groups, a change of level and so on, establish 'tension points'. Use them to obscure a view to produce mystery and anticipation. As you walk through, the tension is released and converted to surprise. If additional features are revealed in your passage through—a whimsical statue or a richly patterned mosaic wall—anything that catches you unawares, then you have surprise.

Changes of Level

Changes of level alter the viewing point and perspective. A single step can alter our perspective and provide a surprising glimpse. Steeply sloping sites provide the possibility of abrupt changes of direction; you can use this design tool to your advantage to create new and exciting vistas.

Vines hanging from an arbour or arch partially obscure the view, hiding what might be in the corner. The mystery encourages closer examination and perhaps a surprise. The gardener can set up these surprises to deliberately manipulate the scene.

Opposite: Doorways and openings are the simplest ways to create a sense of surprise, hiding the view until a transition is made. Open, this Balinese doorway allows glimpses of another section of the garden with a luxurious daybed beckoning. Closed, the effect is more womb-like and mysterious. 'What lies beyond?' is the common thought.

Balance

Balance brings harmony and stability to a garden. Even without understanding why, a balanced garden looks right. Along with rhythm, unity and accent, balance is a principle that comes from art, but is applicable to garden design.

Symmetry

If two equal sides of a garden mirror each other, then they are symmetrically balanced. In theory, they share the same shape, form, plant height, plant groupings, colours and theme. In reality, most formal schemes seem identical but often have slight dissimilarities. A strong central axis, such as a path, is one way to divide a space; the axis may also be imaginary.

Asymmetry

Asymmetrical balance is more complex to explain but it is often something we appreciate without being conscious of it. Things just look right because the different elements that contribute to an asymmetrical scheme have an equal but different type of attraction.

The key to understanding asymmetrical balance is to follow the Japanese system of number and form to achieve a sense of nature simplified and refined. To achieve balance and harmony, objects and plants were traditionally always placed in odd-numbered groups. A single tree is usually balanced by the space around it. Add a second (or indeed any even number) and balance is hard to achieve without symmetry. Symmetry is diametrically opposed to the Japanese view of nature.

Groups of odd numbers—three, five, seven—are hard to place symmetrically but they work asymmetrically. The elements within each group are arranged in a triangular form; the triangle is crucial for perceptions of vertical and horizontal balance. A triangle can be asymmetric and balanced at the same time and is used both above the ground, for example in the shape of a group of shrubs or trees and for placement of plants.

Using Plants to Achieve Balance

Contrasting plants can add harmony. Curved beds on one side can balance with straight lines on another; a shaded area can contrast with a sunny flowerbed.

Opposite top: In a woodland garden, shades of green with a blend of shapes on both sides of the path create a sense of poise and equilibrium.

Opposite bottom: In a Japanese-style garden, balance is crucial. It is achieved by blending different-sized rocks, different plant masses and foliage textures and light and dark spaces. White gravel and open space contrast and balance with the darker planted areas.

Below: Even in a small vignette, this blend of plants, shapes and textures seems balanced. Poa and other grass-like spiky leaves mix with echeveria and cotyledon with rounded, fleshy, succulent leaves.

Plants need to be strategically placed and we perceive this as stable. Dark-coloured flowers and foliage appear heavier than whites and pastels. Fine-textured leaves appear lighter than coarse foliage. A plant with an open habit and leaves may appear lighter than one with small-leaved foliage grown as a hedge. These types of contrasts in a garden can create balance.

Size and form can also be varied in an asymmetrical design. A tall tree needs an equal mass to balance it in a landscape. This could be another erect tree of similar size, or a horizontal feature: a mass of shrubs as wide as the tree is tall will balance a lone tree. It is also a less weighty alternative.

Proportion

The sizes of the individual components or groups of components in a landscape need to fit into the whole landscape harmoniously. One way to achieve proportion is by applying the principle of transition to the size of the various components. For example, a huge gum tree or a massive shrub such as a rhododendron growing out of a narrow planting bed will look out of proportion to the narrow edging and to the garden as a whole. It should bear some relationship in scale to the garden and to its surroundings, especially in small gardens.

Colour and Tone

For many people, gardens are all about colour. Colour can be the most difficult element to use effectively but it has a value way beyond just making a garden look pretty. Colour can impact on our perception of space, making objects appear closer or further away. It all depends on which colours you use and where you place them.

Colour creates mood, character and atmosphere. It can make you feel exhilaration, joy, calm or even unease. Colours are dynamic. They change character when you mix them or take other colours away. Gardeners who understand this will bring extra charm and personality into their gardens.

Dark-coloured foliage plants used extensively will introduce a sombre tone to the garden. Lighter colours, particularly variegated leaves, can lighten the mood, but use them too much and they can look cheap, even brassy.

Changing Colours

Colour schemes for our gardens need not be static. Colours change with the seasons, especially in cooler climates, where deciduous trees provide autumn tones. In a temperate garden, deciduous azaleas provide a white and pink scheme in spring but turn to orange and yellow in autumn, harmonising with deciduous trees.

Colours, Mood and Distance Perspective

Warm colours like red, orange and yellow make an object seem closer to the observer. A wall painted with these colours would seem closer to the viewer and the space between shorter.

Cool colours like blue and green recede. A wall painted with one of these colours would seem further away. The space between viewer and object would also seem bigger.

Cool colours are restful; warm colours express action and can be stimulating. One of the best ways to make use of warm colours is to place them against a green or dark background, for example hibiscus hidden among green foliage. Filtered light or partial shade also diffuses their intensity.

Greys, blacks and whites are considered neutral colours. Use them in the background with bright colours in the foreground. They can create transition from a group of colours, or between different colours within the same spectrum, such as warm and cool colours.

The brilliant leaves of *Cordyline terminalis*, the ti plant of the South Pacific, change colour with the seasons—brighter in winter and duller in summer.

To increase the sense of depth, place dark and coarse textured plants in the foreground and fine-textured and light-coloured plants in the background.

Colour Draws Attention

Colours can direct your attention to a specific area of the garden. A bright display among cooler colours catches the eye, as do light colours against a dark backdrop. White or light tints focus attention and can be useful in areas close to the house such as a patio.

When using colour to direct attention, consider year-round colour not just seasonal colour, as well as the time of day it will be seen. Colours can affect mood in social settings. Dark colours on a patio at dusk or night might be over-whelming and even antisocial, yet work well in bright sunlight.

Top: Dark and light, the yin and yang of oriental design, is about the attraction of opposites. This display garden shows the artfulness of contrasting dark shades such as charcoal or aubergine with brighter, hotter colours. Orange is not often used for wall colours as it is considered too powerful, but the planting in this 'garden room' is restrained and restricted to grey foliage against a blond gravel background.

Right: Get colour from a mix of foliage and flowers. New leaves on box add lime highlights to an otherwise dark planting of ajuga and violets, both of which are dark-leafed and purple-flowered.

Line

Above: This planting is a symphony of strong lines derived from the retaining walls with box hedging and a line of pleached locust trees (*Robinia pseudoacacia* 'Frisia').

Opposite: We can use line in ways other than planting. This slatted fence is strongly linear and the prominent purple paint shade ensures that it is seen as part of the design of the garden.

ine is one of the more structured elements of design. Without line our eyes would have trouble discerning the form of a garden. Lines are like mental traffic lanes leading the eye in certain directions. Lines lead our eyes from place to place along a set route, while calling attention to points of interest along the way.

Line is both horizontal and vertical. The way lines flow together creates rhythm and vitality. Vertical line is evident in changes in the height of tree canopies and in individual plants. Horizontal line occurs in edgings or in a row of plants butting up against lawn or paving. In small spaces line is accentuated by horizontally branching shrubs and by plants trained along a flat plane, as in espalier. The foliage of some plants seems to mesh into layers (like feathers on a bird) and this is a useful, if subtle, way to introduce line in a small garden. *Strobilanthes gossypinus* is one example of this.

The arrangement of plants in ascending heights from the front to back of a border is also an example of line. Paths form curved or straight lines with garden beds and boundaries. All these threads tie a garden together.

The Power of Lines

Lines work on the subconscious. The width, angle or curve of lines in a garden can influence mood, appearance, access and, like rhythm (page 20), the speed at which we move through the garden.

Straight lines tend to be forceful, structural and stable. A focal point at the end of a straight line is seen more readily than at the end of a curved line. Curved or free-flowing lines are more graceful and gentler for the eye to follow. They create relaxed mood, encouraging you to 'chill out' in the garden. Because straight lines are rare in nature, we tend to associate curved lines with naturalness. The dimension of a curve is also significant: long, gentle curves are seen as elegant and restful, while short, wiggly lines are jarring.

Zigzags suggest erratic movement, agitation and urgency. They work well in modern or bold landscapes and where stiff or spiky foliage dominates. Use them in spaces you walk through such as an entrance garden or a garden that connects two spaces.

Thrusting, upright plants such as cactus or delphiniums suggest action and excitement. Yuccas, bananas and cordylines have foliage that splays out. They are the garden's extroverts. They seem to be screaming 'look-at-me, look at me'. They direct the eye upwards and away from the ground.

Horizontal lines are associated with restfulness and, when laid across the line of sight, widen the view. Laid down the line of sight they lengthen it.

Convex horizontals make steps look wider and disperse attention from what is directly ahead. Concave horizontals focus attention to a central point.

Using Line

The line our eye follows is called the 'line of sight'. We can use this to lead us to focal points. The location of a focal point can determine the line of sight. Focal points create views within a garden and are usually placed at the end of straight lines or where they intersect.

Formal gardens use a central axis to direct views, and rely heavily on straight lines. Formal gardens are often found where surfaces are level or where sloping ground has been terraced to create several different level surfaces. It is hard to imagine a straight line on undulating ground.

Informal gardens use curved lines. Broad sweeps and curved planting lines are often designed to focus our attention from one side of the garden, or from the foreground, towards the middle. The focus is usually somewhat to the left or right of centre. A line directed to the dead centre of a garden appears too symmetrical and therefore unbalanced.

Form

Form and line are closely related. Line is usually considered in terms of the outline or edge of objects; form is basically the shape, structure and volume of a plant or mass of plants. Built structures also have form and you should take this into account when designing the area around them.

The concept of form is related also to the size of an object or area. We also talk about form in terms of individual plant growth habits or planting arrangements.

Plant forms include upright, oval, columnar, spreading, broad-spreading and weeping; each of these can also contribute to pattern and texture.

Scale

Scale is simply the relationship between the size of one object and the sizes of nearby objects. It is important to get scale right for a landscape to look balanced and believable. People need to feel the scale is appropriate to them too. In a forest, an enormous tree can engender awe but in a small garden it can simply feel uncomfortable or oppressive. Features like paths and seats need to be presented on a scale that is usable to people. Use trees and shrubs to link nature and humans. In small gardens, use smaller trees in proportion to the space.

Objects that are too large for the space they occupy can appear absurd. Too great a contrast in the size of objects in a small garden causes a similar effect.

Scale in a small garden is mostly about size relationships that work. Scale and proportion are attributes of unity and both are needed for harmony. Most of the time we can tell instinctively when the scale is right or wrong.

Colour is often a simple way to manipulate scale in a small garden. The techniques can be applied to both plant forms and architectural or hard elements. See the section on colour on page 26 to learn how colours can make objects appear closer or further away.

Below right: A suspended steel platform overlooking a small pond makes an out-of-scale statement in this small garden. A very strong frame enabling people to rest on it supports it.

Below left: Scale is deliberately turned on its head here with a bulky table base contrasting with light-as-air café chairs. The high wall of this inner city court-yard dominates the scene, so the Boston ivy on the wall was allowed to extend the full length and tall bamboo was planted to de-emphasise the ugly modern blond brick building behind.

Above: Overscaling works in a small garden. Placing a single large object in the foreground of a small space can give a sense of grandeur unrelated to its actual size.

Right: An overscaled urn used as a water feature dominates the low retaining wall. Both are given prominence—the wall by painting it a vivid pink and the urn because it is bigger than we would normally expect it to be, given the narrow width of the pond.

Texture

The interplay of different textures of leaves, bark and even built surfaces adds another layer of beauty to the garden. Texture is an aesthetic quality rather than a design principle; it can be used to develop design principles such as pattern, proportion, transition, movement, rhythm, surprise and contrast.

The texture of a plant's foliage or bloom is usually described as coarse, medium or fine. Leaves and branches can be smooth, rough, glossy or dull.

Hard surfaces in the landscape include buildings, walks, patios, ground-covers and plants. On roughly textured hard surfaces, light effects or patterns change throughout the day, often creating interesting focal points or pleasing contrasts with other surfaces.

Exploit the possibilities of pattern and texture, particularly the irregularities. Combining plants with different textures, as well as shapes and sizes, builds interest, whereas using plants with, for example, similar leaf patterns—all small, all round or all arrow-shaped—creates monotony. Mix it up a little.

Texture, Pattern and Space

Patterns are an eye-catching element in garden design, particularly when used on a large scale. Textures and colours play an important part in creating beautiful and intriguing patterns. The main function of patterns is to add interest to a landscape. Pattern serves different purposes depending on the application. Pattern:

- delineates space and forms divisions
- can draw your attention to something
- can be used to build structure by repeating shapes in a set order, for example leaf patterns or growth habit
- can add variety by overlaying repeating patterns with different colours and textures
- can also be applied over a whole space.

Pattern is evident in many different national garden styles. Garden rooms, seen in plan view, are a form of pattern on the landscape. The more formal the garden, the more defined is the pattern. Formal gardens of the Italian Renaissance, the French Baroque or Moorish Spain used more formal line and pattern.

As gardens become less formal, texture exercises a stronger influence on mood and serenity. In the English landscape style, the contrast of subtle textures

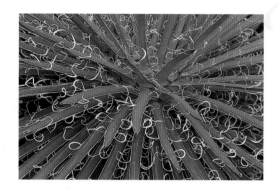

Top: *Dasylirion wheeleri* or desert spoon is a native of arid lands in Arizona, New Mexico and Texas. It grows to about 1.5 metres and is ideal in dry gardens.

Centre: *Haworthia lockwoodii* is a low-growing succulent from South Africa. It grows at altitudes of 500 to 1400 metres and is able to take some cold.

Bottom: The palm-like fronds of palm grass or weevil plant (*Curculigo capitulata* syn. *Molineria capitulata*) grows from South-East Asia to Australia.

exerted a stronger force, as it does in the gardens of Japan. The latter rely heavily on the textural contrasts of stone, foliage, shaped plants and gravel. Modern gardens incorporating smooth stone surfaces, glass and stainless steel rely on similar subtle changes of texture, while maintaining unity of colour and form.

Espaliering adds pattern, and texture varies according to the type of plants used and their growth patterns. Climbing structures and fences can have their own pattern and texture. Pick up any book on Japanese gardens and you'll find an array of textured fences, from solid bamboo to lashed canes, all of which have a strong tactile quality. A pergola casts shadows and can be elegant or stolid, a kind of butch or femme personality in the garden, if you like. Tall thin plants can cast shadows and also enhance line if repeated. Topiary, knots and parterres (traditional low-hedged gardens of the Renaissance) also add texture. Sometimes you may want to touch it but more likely it is the overall pattern you feel an affinity with.

For an outside deck, a wire-framed table, timeless timber flooring and a cosy cowskin cushion provide an array of complimentary textures. The flowers are Gymea lily (*Doreanthes excelsior*).

Time

Pears colour well in a variety of climates from cool to warm temperate. Look for forms of *Pyrus calleryana* such as 'Glen's Form', Chanticleer ®, 'Bradford' or 'Capital' which have an upright form.

Time is a commonly ignored element of design, partly because it is hard to define. It is, however, crucial and easy to anticipate. Taking more heed of it leads to fewer planting and construction mistakes and reduces costs to gardeners.

A garden evolves over time. Trees grow taller and eventually cast more shade. If you haven't planned for this growth, problems generally follow. The canopy may overshadow other trees and shrubs; roots may block drains and lift foundations or paths; and branches may drop, impede traffic or obscure views.

Planning for the effects of time—for example, how weather and climate impact on surfaces, plant growth and maintenance—can avoid potential problems and expense, but it will never completely do away with them. Time has a tendency to throw up unforeseen occurrences, mostly governed by the elements: storm and tempest, hail and wind for instance.

Time also demands the patience and understanding of the gardener. Plants and gardens do not grow overnight. Occasionally they do not grow at all; needing to start over can be discouraging and trying. Even an instant garden (advanced plants installed by a landscaper at great cost) takes time to mature. The mark of a good gardener is tolerance of the dimension of time.

Research is the solution. Look into growth patterns and eventual size of trees and shrubs. Books will give you some information about growth rates and ultimate height of trees but temper the information with scepticism. Many books list the height a tree may attain in its natural environment or in a particular climate, but plants growing outside their natural range behave differently. A rainforest tree in nature, for instance, has different issues to contend with than the same tree commonly grown in a garden. Competition for light, high rainfall and organic-rich soil can force trees to amazing heights, but place them in an open garden bed with shallow, sandy soil, alien weather conditions and competition from other greedy trees and it may only grow into a large shrub or small tree.

The best way to check on the size of any plant is to observe it growing locally. Botanical gardens, large parks, neighbouring gardens and street tree plantings give a better indication of how plants are likely to perform than any book.

Pictured are two recently established gardens that show the importance of time to enjoyment of a garden.

Left: The plants in this small townhouse garden are small at the moment and the perimeters are the dominant feature, but in time they will fill out and the lattice and fencing will be a distant memory. The water feature dominates the young landscape but this will change as the plants mature. The young sasanqua camellias along the fence can be clipped as they grow to retain a sense of scale within the narrow garden space.

Below: The spare, minimalist design of this courtyard matches the modern house renovation. Its limited palette of plants includes three advanced Korean mountain ashes (*Sorbus alnifolia*), a slow-growing columnar form that colours well in autumn and has small white flowers in spring and summer, followed by pinkish autumn berries. Although trees can be overpowering in a small courtyard, the combination of slow growth and erect shape means these will stay in scale for their lifetime, yet also offer the tantalising expectation of a yearly growth cycle. Encased in concrete, as in this Melbourne courtyard, they will remain much smaller than their usual 7–10 metres.

Illusions:
Playgrounds for the Senses

Above: A pergola frames the view. Its vertical and horizontal beams separate out areas, creating different visual zones and enhancing the sense of space. Try funnelling the point of view with denser plantings in the foreground than in the background.

Opposite: A sandstone sculpture by Chris Bennetts of Ishi Buki is set among a series of intersecting lines of pebbles while a stepping stone path crosses them in a sea of dwarf mondo. This creates a theatrical setting, with hedges as wings.

Small gardens rely heavily on optical illusion—tricks of perspective similar to those used by artists. Artists use such tricks to create a sense of three-dimensional depth on two-dimensional canvas; garden designers use similar tricks to make a small garden appear larger.

Garden as Theatre

Ancient Japanese gardeners were masters of illusion. Many of their techniques are now part of the lexicon of modern Western design. The most significant is 'borrowed scenery' or 'shakkei'. Think of the garden as a stage and the view beyond as the scenery on a stage—suggested, imagined and real.

Classically, borrowed scenery meant working a distant scene, such as a mountain or hillside view, into the visual ambit of the garden. In a contemporary Western context, the view is likely to be a district or urban scene, a tree, a tall building or even a distant sports field. Borrowed scenery falls into four classifications. They are:

far—such as a view of a distant mountain

near—such as a tree just outside the fence

high—the view above the fence (a district view, perhaps)

low—the view below a fence or through a window in the fence.

Illusion and Perspective

Here are some ways to create the illusion of depth and space:

- Place a larger object in the foreground, and a smaller one in the background, or place a series of progressively smaller focal points along a path so the smallest is furthest away.
- Build paths that become narrower as they move further away.
- In the background use colours that recede (see Colour and Tone on page 26), for example dull greens, greys, silver and blues, to enhance the sense of depth.
- Place items in the way of a path to force a deviation and create new vistas.
- On level ground, raise the ground level so the path slopes upward and away from the line of vision.
- Build rectangular garden beds or ponds to be narrower at the far end. To the viewer this will read as a distant perspective even in a small space.

- Make raised beds, low walls or hedges lower at the far end to achieve the same effect as above. If there is an open view, such as a stand of trees, make it seem further away by running a hedge or planted screen towards it, tapering the inner sides of the planting lower than the outer edges.
- Use larger paving pieces in the foreground and smaller ones in the rear. This works best with irregular stone such as stepping stones or stone slabs.
- Grade gravel from larger gauge in the foreground to smaller in the rear.

Tricks and Illusions with Plants, Art and Structures

- Frame the distance by creating a tunnel effect with plantings along a path. If plants completely enclose a path, the distance seems much greater. The effect works by reducing the viewing angle to a pinpoint.
- Enclose a small back deck with a trellis festooned with vines. Enclose the sides with perennials or soft-stemmed plants at ground level to funnel the view and trick the eye.

Strongly intersecting lines in this narrow garden stem from its sharp gradient. Steps had to be incorporated into the design to make it navigable, and the angled boundary made the shapes more like parallelograms than rectangles. From above it assumes a rich geometric pattern.

- Use large-leafed plants in the foreground and smaller leafed plants behind. In a tropical garden for instance, plant Abyssinian banana (*Ensete ventricosum*) close to the house where its overscale dimensions help to balance smaller plants behind.

- Trompe l'oeil is a form of illusion. An almost photorealist painted image, for example on a garden wall, can 'extend' the garden beyond its boundaries.

- Mirrors duplicate images and create a false perspective. Two mirrors opposite each other will reflect the opposing view almost to infinity. But beware—mirrors will also replicate undesirable elements like hoses and service areas. Disguise these, or angle the mirrors to exclude them from the view. See also Reflections on page 200.

- Distant objects have a greyish, muted, misted quality. To replicate this, use small, woolly-leafed plants in dull olive or greyish tones in the distance.

- A path that disappears behind plantings or structures will seem to recede further into the distance. To accentuate the illusion, plant bold-textured plants at the turning point where the path curves behind them. Plant smaller leafed ones beyond that point.

- Using the qualities of light and shadow is a much-undervalued technique. Moving from a dark area, such as a tunnel of foliage, to a brighter well-lit space can be like a revelation—the lighter area will seem to increase in size in contrast to the darker area.

- Repetition of one element has a strong impact on perspective. A row of the same species of tree or shrub draws your eye along the line. Accentuate the effect by pruning the trees progressively smaller as they get further away. This works best in a formal layout, but can also work in informal designs.

- Graduate colours of foliage plants in a subtropical or tropical garden to obtain a similar effect. For example, use brighter red tones or variegated ti plant (*Cordyline terminalis*) or Fijian fire plant (*Acalypha wilkesiana*) in the foreground, merging them with pink, whitish and then greenish shades in the rear.

- A single large piece in the foreground can set the rest of the garden in relief and make it seem larger.

- To create an illusion of space, allow a single tree to dominate the foreground, rather than cramming in a big collection of smaller plants.

- A window in a bank of shrubs or in a wall can suddenly open up a vista, creating the illusion of more space.

- Miniaturisation is a technique used in Japanese design. Think bonsai or miniature trained pine tree for a start and then imagine a landscape reduced to a small scale. A rock represents a mountain; a field of gravel becomes a sea; a flat stone substitutes for a ship and a mossy mound symbolises an island. Its value is greatest in an enclosed space, where the viewer is able to visualise the 'reality'.

In a narrow space, a trompe l'oeil scene painted on an opposite wall makes the view from a window more interesting by extending the line of view.

Planning for Outdoor Living

Where did the idea of outdoor living come from? Thomas Church, an American landscape architect working in southern California at a time when millions of American servicemen were returning home from the Pacific war, first espoused it as a new garden model in the 1940s. 'Gardens are for people', he declared, and the idea spread.

The type of garden that evolved from Thomas's drawing board is a product of prosperity. It required cash to develop new leisure spaces and the freedom to do away with subsistence elements (the veggie patch!) of older gardens.

But outdoor living is also part of our heritage in Australia. Even in the 1920s, large gardens like Eryldene in Sydney—with pavilions for taking tea beside the tennis court, verandas for morning coffee and patios for lunching—were typical of many in affluent suburbs.

Because our outdoor lifestyle has changed how we use our gardens, we also have to change the way we plan, plant and potter around in them.

Opposite: Using modern garden materials, this free-standing pavillion at a garden show captures the spirit of a Bedouin tent.

Left: This seaside garden includes a quaint drying area. Sleepers and decomposed granite form the surface and thyme is planted between the two.

Places for Relaxation

The modern garden is a place to relax where once it was a place of 'work'. Storing wood and firing fuel stoves were more onerous than flicking a switch.

Relaxation takes many forms. For some the act of gardening itself is a form of relaxation. That is how it should be. If the garden is a chore, something is surely wrong. Fix it: make it your first priority to analyse and plan a solution. The garden should serve you; you should not be its servant.

Outdoor living blends the comfort of indoors with the freedom of the outdoors, so ease of maintenance is essential. There are four key areas to consider:

1 Position A north-facing position allows maximum sun. Deciduous trees will allow sunlight to enter in winter, and provide shade in summer.

2 Access and transition Maximise the usefulness of your outdoor spaces with direct access from interior to exterior—a seamless transition between inside and outside. Use French, concertina or sliding doors that open directly onto a deck, balcony or patio.

Make an attractive transition between house and garden with a deck devoted to dining and viewing the garden. A long path leads to a focal point at the end of the vista. This garden is narrow and the spilling-over planting along the path gives an illusion of greater depth—a welcome device in all small gardens.

A brilliant solution to lack of space: the steel platform (foreground) provides extra space for guests to stand and, when not needed, retracts under the deck to reveal a water feature.

3 Furnishings To create the illusion of space keep the space open and uncluttered most of the time. To make better use of space, incorporate built-in benches or foldaway furnishings. Bring in extra seating when guests arrive. You can even move indoor furnishings outside when the need arises. Stackable chairs are ideal for alfresco dining. They fit comfortably in the kitchen and are light enough to carry outside when needed for large parties. For light meals for one or two, consider a foldaway table.

Provide inviting places to sit. You may sit on a hard stone bench in a corner of the garden for a few minutes, but for conversation and conviviality, cushions provide maximum comfort; bring them out of storage when needed.

4 Simplify and de-clutter Nothing destroys the ambience of a small garden like clutter. Avoid clutter by providing adequate storage space. Built-in cupboards and benches hide tools and garden essentials but also add a structural element and make a confined space more functional.

To make a small space seem bigger, use large pavers. Pavers 40 x 40 centimetres or bigger look less cluttered than smaller ones. Match pavers to the building style to complement materials used in the house—this helps unify house and garden. Such harmonious pairing also makes an area seem bigger.

Avoid large numbers of small pots, as these are the worst clutterers of small backyards. Instead, create a mini-garden in large containers. Group plants with similar needs in one large pot. Plants benefit from growing in a community and need less frequent watering.

Built-in bench seating saves space in outdoor living areas. Instead of a dedicated outdoor table the owners bring out the kitchen table for alfresco dining. Accessorise. Go for comfort and style. Seagrass cushions edged with silk inserts look sumptuous, are versatile outdoors and can be moved around to suit multiple uses as backrests or cushions.

Finding Solutions

To meet all the needs placed on the modern garden we need to solve the shortage of space and yet retain a clean and uncluttered garden. Part of the answer is to make one unit serve more than one purpose.

Sheds

Packing away the day-to-day objects of life so they are out of sight can be a powerful de-stressing element in a modern garden. There will always be tools to store, no matter how small the garden: garden beds need digging tools, the lawn needs a lawnmower and a hedge needs a trimmer. Tools and other objects increase with time. The usual place for such things is a garden shed. Most are utilitarian, particularly those aluminium ones that dot suburbia. Disguise them with a fast-growing vine, preferably grown on a support such as lattice.

An alternative to the full shed is a narrow lean-to fitted against wall or fence. If you're putting one on a boundary fence, ensure you have the permission of neighbours and any regulating authority. Consider the potential for termites if using timber.

A glance through gardening magazines will reveal many companies selling narrow sheds that fit into niches in walls and similar places. Often called 'buddy' sheds, they are prefabricated, slim and generally unobtrusive.

Sometimes painting a shed can give it new life. One Melbourne company manufactures compact sheds that resemble miniature bathing sheds. Painted in a range of colours they turn the humble shed into a highlight.

Below: A slender 'Buddy' shed fits into a narrow space behind the entertaining area. It has room for garden implements and even a bike. A curved wall in front hides it from general view.

Below right: In this contemporary garden, a lavastone wall separates living spaces from a functional hidden cupboard. This houses gas cylinders for the barbecue, tools and other household necessities. The wall ensures that the space is not visually isolated and is included in the view from the house, adding to a sense of spaciousness.

The shed can also double as an outdoor room/office/workspace. Such a shed will need to be designed by a draftsperson or architect and plans submitted to council. With the increase of home employment, many a small office built at the end of the garden presents another viewpoint for enjoying the garden.

There are long-term possibilities too. For example, the kids' playhouse can be converted to a garden shed when they have outgrown it.

Making Room for Kids

If you have children, a safe and creative place for them to play may be top of your list. For a small terrace or townhouse garden, grass is not really a viable option. Instead, paving provides a useful surface for games with wheeled toys. For the very young, a daily trip to the neighbourhood park with its play equipment and grass should suffice. Fortunately, most inner-city areas have small neighbourhood playgrounds.

Some newer housing estates, although they provide little space for a backyard lawn, have more room at the front. Just be sure that access to roadways is barred and children are supervised at all times.

Sandpits can be designed to transform into planting beds when children grow up. Seating benches alongside make access and supervision easier.

Older children will use a blank wall to play a variety of handball games; a hoop can also be fastened to the wall for basketball.

Small children need a place to play and a sandpit is a good way to ensure that they get their own space. When they outgrow the area, simply dispose of the play equipment and convert the sandpit to planting beds or deck space.

Roles of a Modern Garden

- Drying space for laundry
- Dtorage space for tools
- Space for utilities like air-conditioning units and oil tanks for heating
- Garbage and recycling bin storage
- Kitchen garden
- Dining
- Entertaining
- Playground
- Bike and toy storage
- Open space
- Pot plants

Hiding Utilities

Regardless of size, the garden is as much a working space as a kitchen or bathroom. It contains many functional bits that are not particularly attractive: garbage bins, recycling boxes, drains, pipes, garages, sheds, oil tanks, irrigation control panels, worm farm, compost heap, air-conditioning unit and clothesline.

Small gardens rarely have room for a 'service area', the traditional space for these functions. In larger gardens, it was an area often hedged, fenced or screened from view of the house and the rest of the garden. But in some oddly shaped small gardens, the block creates useful hidden nooks and crannies.

It is not always possible to design a garden from scratch, and often we inherit structures that belong to another age when aesthetics were less important. This is where disguise comes into play.

Many older terrace houses have a long narrow section originally designed for fire protection when kitchens used fuel stoves. Storage units placed at the end or along the wall can often hide some of these elements. Air-conditioning compressors need circulating air, but any good handyman or builder can knock up a slatted frame that hides the unit while still allowing airflow. If it is under a window, some lightweight containers filled with long-term perennials or colourful annuals will present a more pleasant outlook than a dull beige steel unit. If there is room at the base, consider planting a light climber such as old man's beard (*Clematis aristata*) or a happy wanderer (*Hardenbergia violacea*) vine. Neither

is too heavy or dense to impede the unit's operation. If it gets too dense, simply prune it. If there is room to concentrate all of your utilities in one spot, a fenced-off area will hide them effectively.

Many people dispense with the clothesline nowadays in favour of the electric dryer, but there is no denying its usefulness. There are many folding models on the market these days that collapse against a wall and are relatively unobtrusive. An alternative for smaller items is to dry clothes on a couple of folding units. For larger items like sheets and duvet covers, attach a single (or double) strand of stainless steel wire to either end of a courtyard or passageway using a toggle attachment from a boating supplier. The great advantage of this system is it can be unscrewed when guests are coming. It can also double as a support for temporary shade or rain cover. For example, matchstick blinds provide summer shade; a shade sail or heavy-duty plastic sheeting used by cafés will keep rain off.

Use whatever space you have available. For instance, build storage units beneath a raised deck for mowers, folding chairs or other items that are better out of sight. Incorporate seating into a built-in barbecue and use the space beneath as lockers.

Designing Cover

Any outdoor space used for entertaining needs cover or weather protection. In our increasingly cancer-conscious world, we need protection not only from rain but also from UV radiation.

Overhead cover, particularly all-weather protection, greatly improves the useability of outdoor areas. The choice is between permeable or solid, impermeable covers. That leaves us with pergolas, roofs, shade sails and, of course, trees.

Pergolas provide partial shade if covered by a vine. Pergolas allow free flow of air and provide shade but let rain through.

Roofs keep out rain, but if you want light, use polycarbonate sheeting (a transparent material with UV protection). Allow a gap between the house and pergola to allow hot air to escape. An outdoor ceiling fan will also disperse heat.

Trees are like living air conditioners, cooling and reinvigorating the air. They won't keep us dry in a storm but their dappled shade will keep us comfortably cool in summer.

Shade sails provide an attractive sheltered outdoor living or recreation area. Made from high quality UV-resistant material and marine stainless steel fittings, shade sails can be custom made, and fold away when not in use.

Market umbrellas provide temporary shade but to keep them in good condition pack them away when not in use.

Opposite top: The narrow space at the side of many older terrace houses can be used for storage. By installing a high gate painted the same colour as the house, the owners have found a place for the air-conditioning unit, a portable barbecue, the Otto bin and children's toys. This keeps all essential items handy but out of sight.

Opposite bottom: A built-in barbecue, bench and storage unit keep a small garden neat and tidy.

Below: For a contemporary townhouse, a retractable shade awning provides UV protection and keeps out all but heavy rain. It also protects the interior from heat and the bleaching effects of hot westerly sun.

Walls and Boundaries

Few things define a small garden as much as its boundaries. In most cases, small gardens are surrounded on all sides by fences, walls, hedges and buildings.

Walls immediately define a space. They define the shape of rooms and hallways in a house and they do the same in a garden, albeit in different ways. A garden is likely to be more open, with planted areas defining the style and character of spaces. The interaction between different boundaries, flooring materials and plantings can contribute to a well-designed garden.

In a small terrace or townhouse, garden walls are likely to be masonry or at least visually dominant. Old brick or stone walls become part of the structure of the garden and a main feature. Elsewhere, the traditional Australian boundary is the paling fence; often the best treatment is disguise.

Opposite: Sometimes a solid wall is not absolutely necessary to provide a boundary. This black-painted bamboo-slatted curtain hides the view behind and looks dramatic, especially with the red-painted maple stems.

Below: Boston ivy growing on a wall provides seasonal interest by changing form over the year. Here it is in its autumn guise. The courtyard wall is quite high, but a plank of timber suspended from the wall by means of a strong chain provides seating.

Fence Hiders

Vines or creepers grow well on a structural framework such as lattice, trellis or, for a more contemporary feel, along stainless steel wires.

Blueboard is a manufactured concrete product that comes in weatherproof sheeting and, gives the effect of a solid wall. Nail it to the fence or to a separate frame in front of the fence. Apply a rendered finish with a textured paint or simple bagged concrete. It makes possible colour effects not normally available with fence panels. It adds a sense of unity to the garden by removing the narrow gaps in timber fencing.

Trellis panels add height to a garden and enhance the sense of enclosure that is a common feature of small gardens. Adding height increases the range of vines to grow and also hides the neighbours. If the garden is shaded by the fence plants can get up higher into the sunlight.

Paint can also make a fence 'disappear'. Use a drab olive or grey–green, charcoal or bronze to make the fence recede; avoid dark, harsh tones like Brunswick Green, or bright, light colours that will draw attention to a fence.

Bamboo panels are sold in rolls and attach to fences with galvanised nails.

OPPOSITE

Top: The slatted fence and gate leads from this small rear townhouse garden to the front garden. The interior blinds mimic the line of the slats and give the small space a distinct sense of unity.

Bottom left: The wall in an apartment complex is richly planted with variegated star jasmine, clivias and roses making it blend very happily with a neighbouring hedge at the rear. This gives the space a fuller, more spacious feel even though the balcony is quite narrow. There is a larger niche for a table and chairs.

Bottom right: Espalier is a means to getting more plant material into a small space. Here a lemon is espaliered against a mini-orb clad wall to give a Mediterranean feel to a small townhouse garden.

Below: A back patio area is given a complete jungle theme enclosed by dense plantings of rainforest and subtropical plants. It looks like it is built in but the enclosure is achieved purely by planting.

Planting Solutions

Hedges are a good way to disguise fences. They can be used as boundaries within a garden too. The range of plants suitable for hedging is huge, enabling you to use hedges at all levels of the garden, from groundcovers to tree size. Hedge plants include photinia, lillypilly, and sweet viburnum (*Viburnum odoratissimum*).

Pleached *allée* is essentially a hedge on sticks. Instead of allowing the hedge to grow from the base, it takes a tree form, with the trunk a major element of the design. The foliar section is trained like a hedge. Suitable plants include pear (*Pyrus* spp.), *Laburnum × waterei* 'Vossii', hornbeam (*Carpinus betulus*) and macadamia (*Macadamia teraphylla*).

Shrub borders are a traditional Australian way of hiding boundaries. They are essentially an informal treatment but can be used in more formal settings if a single species with a regular habit of growth is chosen. Suitable plants include *Rhondoletia amoena*, *Camellia sasanqua* and *Hibiscus rosa-sinensis*.

Espalier (see page 216) is a technique for training trees (often fruit trees) flat against a wall for fence. It can be ornamental, as well as a practical way to increase yield. Flowering plants such as blossom trees work well and so many different patterns can be created. Suitable plants include apple, pear, citrus, olive and *Camellia sasanqua*.

Don't Skimp on Quality

Landscaping a small garden can be a money saver. With less area to cover on high-end costs like paving and walls and big features like ponds, pools or spas, there is usually a bit of give in the budget to choose higher quality products that might be too expensive over a larger expanse. Better quality fixtures should also translate to using quality installation. Don't skimp on workmanship. There is no value in buying good products and ruining the effect with do-it-yourself laying or construction. Small gardens also focus attention onto a small area so it is important to have a high standard of workmanship.

Garden Flooring

Foot traffic is more concentrated in a small space and lawns rarely stand up to the vigorous wear they sustain. Paving or flooring of some kind is therefore essential in at least part of the smaller garden.

The range of materials varies and there are many considerations to take into account when selecting a garden 'floor'. Start by selecting materials that are appropriate to the location. Paving around pools, for instance, being more exposed, needs to be colourfast, UV resistant, non-reactive to chlorine or salt water, and resistant to damage from tree roots.

Aesthetic considerations are also important. Choose materials that blend with your style of garden. Timber, particularly a mix of sleepers and decomposed granite, works in well with the bush garden; bricks with a cottage style; travertine marble with Mediterranean gardens; and square sandstone or limestone with formal gardens. Large-format concrete pavers look good in modern styles. There are other such combinations so it pays to check them all to make sure what you like is suitable for your garden.

Although budget is usually a major consideration, some cheap alternatives simply do not last. At least in a small garden there is less area to be covered, so you need a smaller quantity of material. This helps keeps the overall price down considerably, making it cheaper to buy premium products with a higher unit price.

Ideally, choose a product that lasts and retains its appeal with age. Stone products are often the first choice but also the most expensive. The alternatives for the budget conscious are concrete products; many are a good match for real stone in looks and endurance.

Stone paving is available in a wide range of finishes, including honed, sawn, combed, chiselled, riven, hammered and punched. For high-traffic areas such as pathways and courtyards, sawn or other smooth finishes are the better choice. Some locations, such as pool surrounds, steps or shady spots where moss and algae grow in winter, demand more heavily textured finishes for better traction.

Above: Sawn bluestone is a traditional material used here to give a slightly oriental feel to the entrance garden of a terrace house. Room was left for a few plants to nestle the house to the surroundings and rounded pebbles help to convey the theme.

Opposite: For a tropical-style garden in a beach suburb, timber boardwalks were an inspired choice. Surrounded by palms, ferns and cordylines it gives the impression of walking through a whole coastal ecosystem.

Colours Choose paving colours that are also used elsewhere in the outdoor area, such as roof, guttering, fencing or house render.

Laying paving The area to be paved must be well drained and well prepared. Most stone paving is laid onto a bed of washed river sand, but thinner materials, such as some slate, terracotta and ceramic tiles, are laid on a mortar or a concrete bed.

Caring for pavers The white bloom on new pavers is called efflorescence. It is caused by salts leaching to the surface. To control it, allow pavers to dry out, then sprinkle slightly damp sand over the surface. The sand absorbs the salt and is then brushed off.

Algal growth is common in shady spots, particularly in winter. Commercial algae removal products will help reduce it. Alternatively use a stiff broom to scrub the area clean.

Apply a glyphosate spray to weeds between pavers to control them. Be careful not to get it on nearby useful plants as they may be badly affected. A more organic and manual control is to use an old knife to cut the roots between the pavers. Boiling water, applied carefully, also kills weeds between pavers.

For a native garden, rough-hewn timber and natural stone make good materials for paths that are not traversed regularly. Here both serve as stepping stones and are interplanted with native violet (*Viola hederacea*).

Stone

Natural stone is the classic paving material. Sandstone, granite, limestone, bluestone and slate are among the popular choices.

Sandstone comes in a wide range of colours originating from many regions of Australia as well as overseas. Indian sandstone has recently become available and is relatively cheap. Sandstone achieves a good patina quickly and always looks good in heritage and cottage gardens.

Slate is available in many colours, from rich red to dark green to silver grey. It is durable and useful where an interior/exterior transition is required. It performs equally well outside and inside and can be sealed to retain its natural colour.

Granite is suitable for high-traffic areas and copes well with salt water (in a pool). It too comes in many colours, from pink to grey, black and brown shades.

Reconstituted and composite stone pavers are made to look like the texture and colour of natural stone. They are made by combining raw materials with concrete casting techniques and products. They are a sturdy, budget alternative to natural stone.

Concrete Pavers

Concrete that makes no bones about being concrete is an honest material and well suited to many modern makeovers. It has a unique, not quite earthy, semi-industrial feel; it can have a distinctly contemporary edge. Concrete pavers are available in a range of colours, shapes and sizes. They are less porous than natural stone, an advantage in shaded or south-facing positions. Large paver sizes have fewer joints and look less busy. This is desirable in minimalist or contemporary styles, giving a smoother, less textured finish. A recommended size is 40 x 40 centimetres and upwards. A combination of square and rectangular pavers can also reduce directional elements in a small space. Thus we are less likely to perceive a tiny yard as either short and squat or long and narrow.

Bricks and Other Pavers

Bricks are moderately priced and look warm and inviting. But because they have a small unit size, they can make a small area look even smaller. One advantage is that they can be laid in many different patterns, from classic stretcher bond (the same way house bricks are laid, with each row offset by half a brick) to herringbone. They are laid on a bed of sand and concreted on the edges to prevent movement.

Clay pavers are made from natural clays and fired at high temperatures. The product is long lasting and colourfast.

Terracotta tiles have fallen from favour a little but are nevertheless a cost-effective and sound option. They range in colour from gold to rich red and have an earthy appeal.

Top: Quartz pebbles laid in a bed of wet concrete make an interesting patterned path.

Bottom: Strips of rumbled pebbles bought commercially look especially attractive laid between large clay pavers, breaking the monotony and creating interesting floor textures.

Bridging the Generation Gap

The never-ending lawn looms large in our collective psyche as the only type of garden suitable for kids, but smart design can turn even the smallest patch of backyard into a playground for both parents and children.

This inner-city garden is located behind a recently renovated terrace. The owners have two small children and wanted a no-fuss, easy-care garden. The resulting space is a smart, uncluttered outdoor room that will grow with the children, proving a garden can be both child friendly and a sophisticated adult retreat.

The garden is formal and structured, with concrete paving. Timber benches, a sand pit/planter and raised water feature are all built-in around the perimeters. The warm tones of timber, and the delicate, loosely foliaged plants soften the design's hard edge.

Making the Most of Space

In order to make the best use of the small space, a built-in bench runs along one wall. A contemporary lightweight breakfast table is easy to lift through the concertina doors for outdoor dining. Adults can sit and read or have coffee, while the kids can play outside. For most of the day, the garden is shaded, providing UV protection without a shade sail.

A Low-maintenance Garden

The owners wanted a low-maintenance garden. The planting design is simple, with bamboo and a potted frangipani. Hardy black bamboo ties in with the neighbours' bamboo visible over the fence. Slate mulch on the surface of the soil conserves moisture and adds a modern edge.

Bamboo is vertical so it doesn't take up ground space; it's

The garden is small but uncluttered because the owners dispensed with the idea of an outside table. The sand pit in the corner can be converted to a garden bed or kitchen garden when the children outlive its usefulness.

Opposite left: The willow wall panel and bamboo soften the wall painted with a rich orange Murobond paint called Papaya.

Opposite right: The water feature sits on large pebbles that are safe for kids.

evergreen and adds sensuality. Bamboo is musical, its branches wave seductively in a light breeze and at night, and it casts intriguing shadows. Most types of bamboo prefer partial shade but some cope with full sun. In a garden bed rather than a container, use clumping, non-creeping bamboos such as Himalayan weeping bamboo (*Drepanostachyum falcatum*) or slender weaver's bamboo (*Bambusa textilis* var. *gracilis*), as neither run amok.

A Safe Play Area for Children

The owners wanted a safe play area for their two young children. However, they did not want lawn and the small space and shade precluded lawn anyway. The design incorporates a sandpit and a large, open paved area ideal for push toys and bikes. The sandpit is cleverly designed to be transformed into a garden bed—perhaps for the children's own garden—when the children outgrow it. Scratch a gardener and you'll find that's how most of us got started. Alternatively, it can be converted to more seating.

The owners were keen to have a water feature, but mindful that children can drown in just a few centimetres of water. So the water feature was placed high out of the children's reach, a good metre above the ground. It is filled with river pebbles to reduce the depth of water.

Screening Out the Ugly

Black bamboo has been used to hide a large warehouse across the back lane, for privacy and aesthetic reasons. Planted in a raised bed, the bamboo screens more effectively than if it were planted at ground level or than the rendered wall alone. Unlike trees, the bamboo won't outgrow the garden (it's entirely enclosed in a galvanised container and nourished by a commercial potting mix) and it needs no pruning or major maintenance.

Above: The water feature is raised and filled with large pebbles as a safety measure.

Opposite: The bamboo is mulched with slate chips which retain moisture and are unlikely to be strewn around or eaten by children, who are prone to putting rounded pebbles in their mouths.

Design Elements

Pattern The human eye cannot follow a pattern in a small space so the geometric style of the pavers works well. There is no directional element is this form of concrete paver so it doesn't add to a perception of widening or lengthening the space. Moisture and shadow give each paver an individual look that can change throughout the day so the paving never looks static or boring. They come in four interlocking sizes, forming a random pattern when laid. Its great advantage is its non-slip surface even when wet and it needs no special treatment or coating, though a sealer could be applied. It develops interesting patterning over time and this only adds to its appeal.

Colour Don't be afraid of it. The bold, almost smoky orange behind the bench seat offsets the neutral stone colour on other walls, adding vitality.

Accessories Stylish, versatile seagrass cushions edged with silk inserts look sumptuous and make comfortable seats or backrests. The large, glazed conical pot used for the frangipani fits with the contemporary style of the garden.

Splurge on art The willow wall panels have a rich, earthy brown patina that adds an organic contrast to the painted walls. Imported from England, these traditionally crafted Somerset fences were originally built as stock enclosures.

Enhance the mood A submersible pond light not only illuminates the fountain but also creates a moving pattern on the wall as the breeze rustles the bamboo. The contemporary bowl is tough fibreglass composite. A glazed pot may need sealing.

Contemporary Zen

The garden is designed as a contemplative space, with the water bowl and Buddha taking centre stage. They are also visible from within. The low coffee table keeps the view from being obstructed.

Courtyards are all about outdoor living. The transition from interior to exterior needs to work well. The advantage of modern townhouse architecture is that the rear wall is usually glass, removing the barrier of a solid wall.

This garden points to a new direction in Australian garden design. Like modern Australian cuisine, our gardens have evolved. Inspiration not imitation moves garden design forward. Blanket imitation has been replaced by fusion, where existing ideas from different cultures are reinvented to meet our own needs.

This courtyard garden serves two functions. One is as an entertainment space—visitors and residents alike can flow between indoors and outdoors. The principle dining space remains indoors and doors opening onto the garden increase the enjoyment of the garden itself.

The second role is to provide a pleasing view from the interior living space in all weathers. If it has sufficient interest, it has the same appeal as a fish tank—inducing serenity through contemplation. This garden has been designed as both a passive and active sanctuary.

The space is roughly rectangular, with a land area equivalent to most townhouse gardens. The courtyard adjoins a common garden in a modern townhouse complex. Guests enter through what is essentially the back gate and walk through the courtyard. It was thus important to establish visual interest both from inside the house and from the entry gate.

A back gate leads to a park outside, which considerably enhances the sense of space. Clumps of bamboo soften the fences.

Capturing Spirituality

This garden captures the spirituality of an Asian garden without a copycat approach. Two varieties of non-invasive bamboo create a bold yet sensual effect. Slender weaver's bamboo (*Bambusa textilis* var. *gracilis*) evokes a tone of masculinity, while the graceful Himalayan weeping bamboo (*Drepanostachyum falcatum*) creates a feminine balance.

A large stone font beneath a wall-mounted Buddha contains water and is highlighted with low-voltage garden uplights. The Buddha is the garden's major focal point and enhances the sanctuary element of the garden.

Optimising Entertaining Space

The design maximises entertaining space by removing the need for a dedicated outdoor table. The glass wall and internal arrangement means that food can be cooked alfresco on the barbecue and eaten inside, while the diners retain a strong visual connection with the outdoors. The view of trees outside the courtyard uses a time-honoured Japanese concept of 'borrowed scenery': by bringing the view beyond the fence into the main composition, the small garden assumes greater depth.

Flooring to Hide a Drain

A large drain runs through the middle of the courtyard and this had to be accessible for maintenance but not visible. To cover the drain, timber decking was laid over the existing quarry tiles. This gives the space aesthetic unity but removes the hard edge of the previous landscaping. It looks warm and feels good underfoot. Combining tiles and timber decking adds a dynamic sense to the flooring. The dark colour of the decking and the outside furniture repeat the colours of the inside fittings, blurring the distinction between internal and external and making both seem larger.

Improving Plantings and Fencing

Landscaping had been installed by the developers and was filled with standard nursery lines. An ugly brushwood fence, part of the strata property, could not be removed. Two Chinese tallowwood trees (*Sapium sebiferum*) outside the boundary fence shaded the garden and their aggressive roots invaded it.

Low-maintenance but softer textured plants, such as bamboos and grasses, replaced the original plants. The original brushwood fencing was clad with bamboo, creating an instant oriental feel. It opened up the space and changed the ambience. Root-control barriers were installed to avoid future problems from the trees outside the fence.

Saving Space

Where space is limited, give functional elements a dual role. The owners' wish list included seating, a water feature and locating the barbecue in a well-ventilated spot. They are also keenly involved in maintenance of the common garden area outside the fence and needed storage for garden tools.

A built-in bench seat with tool storage and cupboards along the side fence saves space, instead of freestanding outdoor furniture. The cupboard conceals the gas regulator and acts as a bench for the barbecue. The bench top is tiled with the same flooring tiles for continuity. The benches and seat are compact and blend into the overall theme. Having tools handy is also an incentive to spend a quick 15 minutes in the garden.

Plants

Slender weaver's bamboo (*Bambusa textilis* var. *gracilis*) is a graceful, frost hardy bamboo growing to 6 metres, making it useful as a dense screen. It is a clumping type and does not become invasive.

Himalayan weeping bamboo (*Drepanostachyum falcatum*) is a dwarf clumping bamboo to 4 metres. It prefers shade and a cool, sheltered climate although it is remarkably tolerant of mild subtropical conditions.

Gardenia 'Florida' produces small flowers mostly in two flushes—November and March—with spot flowering through most of the warmer months.

Phormium 'Anna Red' is a hybrid form of New Zealand flax that copes well with warm climate zones and normally high summer rainfall.

Chinese silver grass (*Miscanthus sinensis* 'Sarabande') is a variegated form growing more than 1 metre tall. During warmer months the leaves have a wide central silver stripe; in winter they die down.

Leather-leaf sedge (*Carex buchananii*) grows to 50 centimetres tall and wide. It has curled-over tan-brown leaves that many assume are dead; it is best used for foliage contrast.

Chinese tallowwood (*Sapium sebiferum*) is a deciduous shade tree that colours well even in warmer areas.

Moses-in-the-cradle or Rhoeo (*Tradescantia spathacea* syn. *Rhoeo discolor*) is a semi-succulent plant that needs good drainage but thrives in frost-free locations.

Dancing or Spanish lady orchid (*Oncidium* cultivars) resents overwatering, a common cause of death with exotic orchids. They need winter rest (let them dry out a bit).

Lily turf (*Liriope muscari* 'Variegata') suits sun or half-shaded spots as an edging.

Goldfussia (*Strobilanthes anisophyllus*) has dark, almost black leaves in sunshine, with small mauve flowers.

Sacred lotus (*Nelumbo nucifera*) grows well in a large container, provided it has room to spread and receives plenty of sun.

Calathea species and plants of related genera (*Ctenanthe*, *Stromanthe* and *Maranta*) are good groundcovers in moist, warm gardens.

Left:: Ornamental grasses are used for character. *Miscanthus sinensis* 'Sarabande' and *Carex buchananii* create seasonal interest and *Phormium* 'Anna Red' has a more permanent sense among the ever-changing perennial grasses.

Below: All the accoutrements of modern living are packed away in these simple cabinets. Chairs, barbecue and garden tools are hidden from view but easy to reach when needed.

Styled
Spaces

Style has a close connection with the functional side of gardening. Design fuses style and lifestyle. It brings personality, tastes and skill levels together to create a practical, achievable garden. It involves considering how a garden will look over the passage of time, and anticipating changes. A style that demands too much attention from its owners will not work, even though they might initially believe they have realised their dream.

This chapter looks at some types of gardens and how the different design elements work to create style.

A Sense of Place

We tend to use the term 'style' to refer to many things—formal style, English style, Japanese or Balinese style—as if we need to import, impose or introduce a 'look'. These are more themes than styles. Style relates to how well they are executed.

Choosing a themed garden is fine and we can adopt different degrees of theming. Selecting a theme and carrying it through can be a form of homage, but it can also become parody or caricature.

Take the common perception of gardens lumped under the title 'Japanese'. There are many forms of Japanese garden, from Zen gravel gardens and teahouse gardens to 'borrowed landscape' styles ('borrowed landscape' refers to what you can see beyond the limits of the garden). Each type of garden encompasses many stylised elements rooted in Japanese culture. Western gardeners often misinterpret these elements and impose them haphazardly. Similarly, the decorative elements of Balinese gardens have significance to followers of Hinduism and it can be culturally insensitive to introduce them into an Australian garden without understanding their significance.

A better option, if not fully versed in the psyche of other national spirits, is to adopt an 'influenced by' approach. Adapt appealing elements to your surroundings and situation. You could take as your starting point the serenity of the Japanese tea garden, the austerity of the Zen landscape or the lushness of the tropical Balinese garden—but adapt it to the Australian sensibility, lifestyle and plant palette. We tend to overlook the fact that these styles are the 'native' gardens of other nations.

The phrase 'a sense of place' sums it up. Design and style should create a seamless transition between the garden and the outside landscape. Without this synergy, a themed garden can seem like an imposition, a freak or a visual intrusion.

Quite often in a larger garden, the surrounding trees, houses and landscape make an 'authentic' replication of theme impossible—or at least implausible. It may clash with its surroundings, where a lighter touch would not. In a small garden, one that is enclosed or secluded, where the wider world does not impinge greatly, it is much easier to get away with a full-scale replica.

Whichever path you choose, whether it's replication or adaptation, treat your location respectfully and it will repay you with a garden that is at peace with both you and the surrounding environment.

Above: A stone path through well-kept lawn and a grove of birches establishes an ambience that is reinforced once the viewer reaches the deck and its surrounding pond.

Opposite: A small, enclosed courtyard off the main living area is enlivened by lush plantings of ferns, hydrangeas in pots and subtropical delights such as pitcher plants, orchids and cordylines.

Traditional—
Urban Woodland

A classic approach to garden design does not seek to impose a look on a space. Instead, it allows the design to emerge from the site and uses a traditional planting palette suited to the local climate. Depending on the location, plants selected should be durable and hardy in your local climate, whether tropical, subtropical, temperate or dry.

Located at the rear of a semi-detached house in bayside Melbourne, this garden blends a casual lifestyle with elegant styling. Here, the winter climate is tempered by its maritime location—temperatures can be cool, but are not harsh or cold. The garden uses a palette of cool to temperate plants that perform well under local conditions.

The house is at the end of a row and the garden has a gate onto the side street. A two-storey building at one end serves as garage-cum-study. The design allows for garden viewing from both the house and from the upper-level office window.

Maintaining Access and Spaciousness

It was important to maintain access to the side gate without imposing barriers that made the space seem smaller. This was achieved by creating two distinct zones separated by a long, rectangular pond flush with the slate paving. A generously proportioned pathway to the gate adds a sense of spaciousness without imposing a visual boundary. On entering the gate, a low border of *Liriope muscari* 'Evergreen Giant', arum lily and a dwarf Japanese maple (*Acer palmatum* 'Dissectum Purpureum') creates a visual barrier from the street. Glimpses of the garden are visible but not all is revealed at once. The border creates a sense of mystery.

All-round Good Garden Views

The garden had at least three main vantage points, each of which required a different treatment to enable the garden to read as one. As well as the side entry, the garden was seen from the main entry at the back of the house and from the separate upstairs study—there could be no 'back' of the garden.

The garden developed around a series of rectangular grids: the side passage, the rectangular pond, a large seating area and a rear terrace where the lay of the land stepped down towards the garage. They divide the space into recognisable functional areas. A series of wide-stepped terraces leads up from the garage, reading as an invitation to enter the garden.

This is not a garden of naturalistic curves. From the upper vantage point the grid design forms a coherent pattern of paving, pergola and planting. It shows that a geometrically inspired garden can be softened with plantings that do not need to follow a formal, symmetrical design.

Top: The view from the house shows the garden in the context of its surroundings with a guest house/office-cum-garage at the bottom of the garden.

Above: The colour theme is subtle, with soft lavender grey walls a perfect foil for the mauve rhododendron flowers. Birches, hellebores and white azaleas confirm the woodland feel of the planting.

Viewed from the side entranceway, the garden is seen as an idealised woodland with deciduous trees such as maples and elms and a massed planting of arums and lily turf. The rectangular pond divides the rear entrance from the main entertaining and viewing area of the space. It is reminiscent of the garden pools of the Spanish school, here translated to a softer climate.

Design Elements

Materials Slate flooring used throughout the garden holds the design together. Mixing materials can be visually exciting but it also may fragment a small space. The slate, with its blend of greenish and sandy tones, provides a visual tie with the pale green walls.

Balance and unity The planting contributes to a sense of unity. All are of temperate origin and contribute to a woodland feel in what is a very urban garden. The use of space is contemporary but the planting is traditional, a blend of foliage colours and textures, with a balanced mix of evergreen elements and deciduous trees and shrubs.

Texture While the planting is not complicated, it has variety of colour and form. Strappy-leafed liriope, the large soft leaves of arum, the weeping stems of birch and maple and the upright form of Chinese tallowwood (*Sapium sebiferum*) work well together. Differences in foliage colour or floral exuberance add interest and excitement to the garden.

Space The area is not large but is divided into planted areas and outdoor living areas. Visually compatible trees, shrubs and edging plants help differentiate functional and visual sectors such as the dining room, the woodland walk and the boundary planting. Several changes of level and points of view have been intelligently handled so the garden reads as a three-dimensional piece. In theatrical terms it is a theatre in the round not a lyric theatre.

Light and shadow The small deciduous trees keep the garden cool in summer, their dappled shade adding interesting light patterns to the garden. The shadows also create depth—dark spots seem to recede. The contrast between light and shade helps create a perception of more space.

Structure Using plants as partial barriers to divide the space does not make the space seem smaller—it reads as a unified whole. Hard barriers such as walls or fences could have broken up the space.

Boundaries Shrubs disguise the boundaries on one side and blend with neighbouring trees to extend the space visually. On the streetside boundary, the bed extends along the fence but is given depth when viewed from the dining table by the low border facing the pond. So in place of the borrowed scenery of neighbours' trees, the eye is directed downwards and then upwards. The urban view becomes one of planting and blue sky, not houses and adjacent school buildings.

Above: The upper level of the garage offers a good view of the structure of the garden, with the long, narrow lily pond dividing the living spaces from the rear entrance path. Changes of level and beds established on a grid pattern mark out zones for group dining. A cup of coffee for one is possible. The planting is quite varied in such a small space. Maintenance levels are low to moderate. Some trimming and pruning may be needed as trees grow and mature but the plants are suitable for their climate and require little maintenance other than occasional watering and feeding once or twice a year. Leaves need collecting in autumn but can contribute to mulch and composting.

Opposite top: Rhododendrons thrive in a cooler climate and need rich loamy soil.

Opposite bottom: Easy-to-grow clumping perennials such as arum lilies, *Liriope muscari* 'Evergreen Giant' and hellebores require little maintenance and look good for a long time.

Small Space Tips

Lawn Avoid lawn in a small garden that is trafficked regularly. Walking over lawn can create unsightly tracks in the grass that are difficult to disguise in winter.

At a Glance

Complexity Low
Ability Design professional
Maintenance Moderate

Formal Gardens: Pushing the Boundaries

Formal gardens appeal to our sense of order. They are regular and predicable in an often volatile and chaotic world. Think of a formal garden and words like methodical and orderly come to mind. They are controlled, restrained, labour intensive and precise, but you don't have to be a control freak to love them.

Geometry is a feature of all formal gardens. It stems from one of humankind's most enduring passions—regulating nature. Lovers of formal gardens enjoy the defined symmetrical lines, beautifully manicured lawns and standardised or topiary plants.

Formal gardens have one advantage over all other styles of garden. They tend to look as crisp and fresh after a few years as they did when they were first planted. This is both a plus and a minus. Some may see it as static, but in a small garden the potential to maintain maximum visual impact without the vagaries of seasonal change can be a plus. No other style has the potential to give an unerringly perfect display at all times of the year, from winter through to summer. It comes down to personal taste.

This L-shaped garden fits beside a renovated end terrace and surrounds a conservatory-style extension. This large, glass-walled room has a more colonial ambience than the term conservatory suggests, and forms a wing off the original two-storey terrace. From inside, there are views into every nook of the garden.

The whole garden space is angled obliquely following the road. To deal with this angularity, the garden design follows an almost zigzag pattern, with another L-shape—a formal above-ground lotus pond—set into the furthest corner.

Lotus seed capsule.

Maintaining Variety in a Formal Design

One of the problems of a small garden, and indeed of formal designs in general, is the one-look-and-you've-seen-it-all effect. It's one of the greatest no-nos in garden design. Any garden in this space could easily have fallen into that trap—but it doesn't. A pocket of lawn mimics the zigzag pattern, with more zigzags incorporated into the shape to give it greater depth and interest. So no matter how quickly you intend to look, you are still drawn in by the pattern and the clever variations in different corners.

The interior–exterior transition is a crucial element in modern architecture and garden design. Here, the living room is constructed in the landscape and the garden has become part of the interior design. It is a holistic approach that brings the garden and living patterns together.

Disguising the Fence

At one point, the windows look out onto a narrow south-facing strip of land between the house and the boundary wall. The land alongside is little more than a pathway wide, but the wall needed to be disguised.

To give height and privacy, the owners planted a row of macadamia trees grown as a pleached *allée*—a row of hedged trees. The trunks are displayed like a tree and the foliage trained at a higher level than in a normal hedge. Pleaching is popular in Europe and mostly familiar to Australians from

cooler climate gardens, where linden, hornbeam or beech are the most commonly used trees. It is a technique employed as a screen and, rarely, for shade. The original owners of the property had a macadamia plantation and what better reminder than to plant a hedge of it. Even though the trees are precisely clipped, they still flower and bears nuts.

Beneath this shady hedge, exotic clivias flower in winter or early spring. They are hidden behind low hedges of box, cut square, with a series of living bosses or mounded domes to give it an element of individuality and surprise.

The very complex ground pattern is here seen to advantage. The zigzag corners help to add interest and are an illusion in themselves, helping to make the space look much bigger. The L-shaped construction of the garden around the pavilion-style living room gives the garden depth, as does the staggering of the overscaled potted figs.

At a Glance

Complexity High

Ability Design professional

Maintenance High

Opposite: The topiary figs (right) are *Ficus macrocarpa* var. *hillii* and the pleached *allée* (left) is formed from macadamia nut trees— an unusual but effective use of this plant. . The table doubles as an art installation when not in use but it is a simple job to add a few tables to make it cosy indeed. The raised pond (right) is L-shaped as an echo of the garden itself. It is deep enough for lotus (*Nelumbo* spp.) to grow in it.

Design Elements

Theme The zigzag shape and slight changes in pattern add variety to a classic theme, creating mystery, surprise and dramatic tension.

Structure Hedges, pleached shapes and topiary lend structure to the garden throughout the year. Varying the heights and textures of hedges (the latter achieved by using different species) gives the garden a less static feel, as does the variety of leaf textures.

Boundaries The boundaries are concealed by cleverly planting unexpected trees, such as macadamias grown as a pleached hedge. They are tough, easy to maintain and regrow readily when trimmed into a narrow plane.

Container plants Topiary figs give added balance and texture to the rectangular shaping of the beds. Potted trees always need watering, as containers have a restricted root area, which dries out quickly. Native *Ficus* species seem to cope with less water than many of the more tropical South-East Asian species and Hill's weeping fig (*Ficus macrocarpa* var. *hillii*), a vigorous species, is relatively benign in a pot. It needs periodic root pruning to stop it cracking open its pot and to restrain its growth. With containers this size, this is at least a two-person job and one that could be left to professional gardeners. Root pruning is a technique common in bonsai culture but it is also useful for large topiary or plants that would otherwise outgrow their pot. The roots can be trimmed with a sharp knife, pruning saw or chainsaw. In the ground, it is a whopping great tree, lifting roads and foundations. In a pot, it is not.

A Contemporary Garden

Contemporary garden style is about creating uncluttered havens in the backyard. A contemporary garden can be pared down and simple, yet still have the human touch. There is a tradition of minimalist gardens that are far from cold, for example the sublimely contemplative Zen gardens of Japan.

Colour is the most important element of this contemporary garden. The garden provides a dramatic entryway as well as a secluded outdoor entertaining space. The transformation used low-maintenance plants in basic black.

When the house was renovated to a modern open-plan style, the old, cluttered front yard needed a complete revamp to reflect the changes to the building's architecture. With a new entry gate and garage facing the street, the pool is now entirely private.

From the front garden, a long walkway steps down from the street. This is the most eye-catching part of the garden, with brightly coloured walls, bold plants and a long water feature along the wall. A combination of chartreuse and watermelon pink with a collection of black foliage plants gives it an edgy glamour. Black foliage is best viewed close up, as from a distance it can create a black hole. Here, they are perfect because the passageway is narrow and restricted. The plants are also silhouetted against bright colours for extra drama.

A bright pink feature wall is fitted with three waterspouts. These are Balinese flower shapes carved in soft paras stone, which hardens with age. These spouts deliver a stream of water to the narrow pond planted with waterlilies. Hardy goldfish control mosquito larvae in summer.

Design Elements

Colour Contrasts of light and dark foliage. Bright flowers or light-coloured materials show off the black foliage.

Line and repetition The pool area and the entrance beside it are largely secluded and separate entities. The long line of black foliage directs attention towards the house and screens the pool. It creates impact. Most black-leafed plants are not large and are best repeated.

Plants

Mass-planted *Colocasia* 'Black Magic' picks up the colour of the chartreuse wall, creating a dramatic entrance. Like all 'elephant ears', this plant loves water and will also grow in ponds. The best place for it is where sunlight can dance across the foliage or light the leaves from behind. West-facing afternoon sun gives the leaves a deep mahogany glow.

Five-finger or puahou (*Pseudopanax arboreus*) is a small shrubby tree from New Zealand. The leaves have 5–7 leathery leaflets with serrated margins. Flowers are greenish white to pink tinged. Sweetly scented, they are held in clusters followed by black fruit. They follow the planting theme of bold, dark-leaved plants that is continued in other alcove plantings.

Cordyline 'Nigra' is narrow and erect, just right for narrow spaces. It grows 1.5–2 metres tall and tolerates most conditions. *Acorus gramineus* 'Ogon' below contrasts, with yellow-variegated grassy blades.

Above and opposite left: The space is devoted to a pool so the planting area is quite small. For a dramatic effect, *Colocasia* 'Black Magic' was planted along the path, a good foil for the chartreuse colour of the wall behind it.

Opposite right: Louisiana iris and water lilies turn a narrow raised pond into a flowering planting bed when blooming starts—in late spring for the iris, continuing right through until autumn for the waterlilies.

At a Glance	
Complexity High	
Ability Design Professional	
Maintenance High	

A Coastal Gem

Australians have always been daunted by the prospect of gardening by the sea. We stick to what we know, with alien lawns and plants that look out of place and behave accordingly. But local coastal natives thrive in windswept, salty seaside conditions, with minimal human intervention. With just a little tidying they can become the basis of a beautiful, low-maintenance garden, just the ticket for weekenders and holiday houses.

This sandy courtyard forms a small section of a larger coastal garden on Victoria's Mornington Peninsula. The garden sensitively blends indigenous plants with exotics in the outdoor living area. The garden thrives on natural rainfall and no irrigation.

Close to the house, a generous outdoor living area has been covered with granitic sand rather than pavers, to enhance the beach feel. This may not be appropriate in all locations but it's an example of an alternative to hard paving and a way to make a garden blend with the environment. To maintain a coastal feeling, retaining walls are constructed of weathered, recycled piers, and garden walls from dry-packed limestone. Flotsam and jetsam, the found objects of the beach, remind us of the garden's location.

Subtleties abound, like the fan patterns that remain in the sand when the leaves of grasses are constantly blown across it by the wind.

For a beach garden, the absence of lawn is a plus. Instead, a mulch of sand and collected detritus in the form of shells and washed glass add interest. Chalk sticks and cotyledons grow well in this sandy medium.

Styled Spaces

Blending with the Natural Environment

The garden is not located in a suburban tract but fits into a coastal heath. In order to have it blend seamlessly into the natural environment, the planting palette was kept deliberately simple. A few exotics add colour and form close to the house. Further away, the garden becomes more indigenous and naturalistic. To provide a firebreak, there is some clearing with native plants retained. Instead of a dense thicket however, a ground covering of granitic sand is interspersed with topiarised moonah, the local tea tree, and she oak. This adds a formalised element, visual interest and an interesting counterfoil to the natural backdrop.

Coping with Drought

With no artificial irrigation on site, plants need to survive through the summer dry period. Tanks collect rainwater from the rooftop. Swales and runnels direct water to garden plants when it is available. Growing plants hard forces roots to delve deep for moisture, and sensible plant selection ensures most survive on what nature provides.

The living space is a confined area near the house. Local sandstone walls divide sections. This garden is actually quite large but is broken into smaller units by dividing areas with walls and planting boundaries. These provide a useful model for small coastal gardens.

The entrance garden is filled with tough coastal plants, including succulents in pots, lomandra and echium with its colourful purple spring flowers.

Old sleepers make ideal retaining walls when cut and stood on end. These form steps and walls. The planting is a mix of succulents and indigenous plants found naturally on site.

A blend of native and exotic plants works well with the Aboriginal totem linking the garden with a different heritage.

Design Elements

Materials Close to the building, concrete slabs take much wear and tear and form a link between inside and out. Local decomposed granite forms a hard surface and looks like beach sand—ideal for a coastal feel. Local limestone on the walls forms a strong visual link with the natural colours of the landscape. Seashells, used as mulch and also spread around, enhance the connection with the sea. Recycled and natural landscaping materials integrate the garden with the natural environment.

Boundaries Rough branches form a dividing fence between sections of the garden without becoming a barrier. Placed about 20 centimetres apart, they don't block the view. Their presence simply creates mystery through partial enclosure.

Texture Weathered pier beams with the silvery grey patina of long exposure make up steps and paving.

Plants

The plants chosen need little maintenance. Natives, some clipped into formal shapes, make up the bulk of the planting. Among them are drooping she oak (*Allocasuarina stricta*) and a coastal tea tree known locally as moonah (*Melaleuca lanceolata*). Informal clumps of native spear grass and *Lomandra* species break up the monotony of the sandy surface.

Succulents are easy to care for and come in a range of interesting forms and colours. *Cotyledon orbiculata* has large orbs

At a Glance

Complexity Low

Ability Enthusiastic amateur

Maintenance Moderate

Rough-hewn stakes from local plants make a rustic fence, resembling totems.

of silvery leaves that glow in the moonlight. Senecio adds blue–grey colour and echeverias thrive in pots.

Black- to green-leafed forms of *Aeonium* add structure and architectural shape and have large, pyramidal yellow flower heads. *Euphorbia wulfenii* subsp. *characias* has contrasting lime-green flower heads. Blue spikes of Pride of Madeira (*Echium candicans*) flower in spring and add a colourful contrast to mixed colours of New Zealand flax (*Phormium* cultivars).

Coastal Zen

Japanese gardeners search hard to find the beauty in a gnarled branch, a poetically twisted stem or a few lissom leaves. The Australian coastal flora is filled with plants that naturally look aged and venerable. The twisting, curving branches of banksias or tea trees look just as fine as the antique trees of the bonsai masters of Japan, when revealed by judicious pruning.

Simply select a branch for its shape and graceful appearance, then trim off extraneous twigs along its length. Resist the urge to lop the long and graceful branches, which only results in a mass of feeble shoots emanating from an ugly stump.

Small Space Tips

Garden rooms A larger space is an opportunity to provide garden rooms. Siphon off a sector of land close to the house to create an intimate space for friends and family.

Found objects can enhance a garden, particularly if they come from the local environment.

Small Native Gardens

A water fern unfurling.

The rock lily (*Dendrobium speciosum*) has been renamed *Thelychiton speciosa* by some experts but acceptance is not universal.

Versatile Australian native plants have many great qualities. You can choose the familiar bush look or create a more contemporary look, with clean, geometric lines.

Native plants are perfectly adapted to our climate and soil conditions. They grow in many different environments with an enormous range of climatic and geographic diversity. Plants suited to local conditions are easy to maintain as well as being a valuable food source for many Australian birds.

Low-maintenance Plants

Natives were once heralded as low-maintenance plants. And in the right climate and soil, they are. But like all garden plants they need some attention in the form of light pruning and regular mulching. Neglect these simple tasks and plants become straggly and woody.

Drought Tolerance

Apart from some rainforest species, most native plants are adapted to dry periods but nothing really thrives in drought! For best results, water weekly and provide good drainage. Thick mulch will save on water bills and supply nutrients.

Exotic Mixers

As highlights in an exotic garden, natives are a boon. For winter flowers, few plants can match wattles. Use grevilleas for year-round colour; they also mix comfortably with conifers or tropical plants, depending on the type of leaf. If you want something slightly more manicured try some of the newer lillypilly cultivars. They take clipping, shaping and even root pruning if you want to try bonsai. Lillypillies are good with camellias, woodland plants and strappy-leafed exotics like *Cordyline* 'Red Sensation' or yuccas.

Lomandra is a useful and hardy tufty plant for native gardens and here it works well with yellow rock lily (*Dendrobium speciosum*).

Design Ideas with Native Plants

- Create drifts of colour with masses of one plant. Groups of three to seven have more impact than a solitary bush, especially in small gardens.

- Use colours wisely. Team them for harmony and contrast. White highlights other colours, particularly very bright tones.

- Avoid planting in ones and twos and choosing too many different species. Block planting can look more unified and ordered. Fill in with contrasting shapes and colours. Choose hardy species and repeat the same plants throughout the layout.

- Plan your display over all seasons. Don't just go for spring flowers.

- Include some year-round bloomers like grevilleas. Exceptional performers are 'Robyn Gordon' and 'Honey Gem'.

- Use natives in traditional ways. Try coast rosemary (*Westringia fruticosa*) for hedging or formal clipping. Dwarf *Babingtonia virgata* (formerly *Baekea virgata*) is naturally low and rounded and looks stunning along a sunny path or border.

- Balance trees with shrubs and groundcovers. In a small garden, larger shrubs provide height and colour. Too many trees can overwhelm lower storey plants.

- For extra colour, use native annuals and perennials. Try the many excellent hybrid daisies in the *Helichrysum* and *Brachyscome* families.

- Grow a few plants in pots. Swan River daisies (*Brachyscome iberidifolia*) look good in sunny corners, bird's nest fern (*Asplenium australasicum*) in the shade. If you wish, experiment with boronias and more finicky plants. Outside of southern Australia, try Sturt's desert pea (*Swainsona formosa*) in tall containers filled with a free-draining potting mix and keep out of excess rain.

- Know how big plants will grow before planting out. Unlike exotics, most natives are difficult to transplant except when very young. A mistake usually means starting over with a brand new plant.

Native Cottage Garden

Conventional wisdom suggests that natives are not suitable for small gardens. Many natives need a sunny aspect to thrive, and small gardens are often shaded, for example by overhanging trees. The solution is to choose plants that adapt to these conditions.

This is a suburban Melbourne cottage-style garden using Australian native plants. The odd-shaped block is the result of subdivision of a much larger plot of land. There are different plantings in the front, side and back gardens to accommodate the different aspects that result from buildings and fences casting shadows.

A Shady Native Garden?

The front garden is dominated by a non-native pin oak (*Quercus palustris*). The size of the pin oak imposes many restrictions on the space. In winter it is deciduous, allowing sunlight to filter through to the ground. In summer, the area is shaded. These conditions are alien to most Australian plants as there are few deciduous trees. (A notable exception is Tasmania's Antarctic beech, *Nothofagus moorei*). Plants that can cope with part shade and filtered sunlight in summer have been chosen for this garden. The winter sun is weak, so the plants do not burn or suffer. It is an ongoing process to discover plants that will grow in the shade of this mighty tree. The owner did not want to remove it, so has selectively thinned the plants to allow more light to penetrate.

A line of tree ferns (*Dicksonia antarctica*) anchor the front garden to the house and thrive in the shade.

At a Glance

Complexity Low

Ability Enthusiastic amateur

Maintenance Moderate

The rear garden is a collection of different plants, many of which are heathland varieties not commonly found in general nurseries. Specialist native nurseries stock them as a rule.

A Sunny Back Garden

The back garden is sunnier, and this is where many of the Western Australian plants grow, including kangaroo paws, grevilleas and tea trees. In this cottage-style planting, many plants are grouped together to form a colourful, long-lived display. A narrow path wends its way through. Old logs have been laid on the soil to discourage blackbirds from digging.

The garden is viewed from inside through a sliding glass door. Low-growing or heath-type plants grow in the foreground, with shrubs behind, where they help to hide fences and are able to grow taller to reach the light.

Native Plants that Cope with Shade

False baeckea (*Astartea fascicularis*)

Brachyscome 'City Lights'; *B. multifida* 'Pink', 'Amethyst' (in pots)

Boronia chartace, B. muelleri, B. pilosa

Dampiera species

Diplarrena latifolia

Isopogon anemonifolius 'Little Drumsticks'

Orthrosanthus multiflorus

Prostanthera sericea; P. 'Ballerina'

Scaevola 'Purple Fanfare'

Thelionema umbellatum

Oak-leaved thomasia (*Thomasia quercifolia*), *T. solanacea*

Sun-loving Natives for a Cottage Look

Anigozanthos 'Bush Ranger'

Boronia heterophylla, B. pinnata, B. serrulata 'Aussie Rose'

Callistemon 'Reeves Pink'

Crowea 'Poorinda Ecstasy', *C.* 'Australian Green Cape'

Epacris longiflora

Ozothamnus ledifolius

Hibiscus heterophyllus lutea

Leptospermum 'Cardwell'

Tetratheca ciliata, T. thymifolia

Natives and Honorary Natives

Gone are the days when natives had to be grown in isolation. The trend now is to mix and match—for example, natives with exotics, or succulents with indigenous. The results are exciting and different and point us in the right direction for Australian gardens in the future.

This garden uses a core planting of Australian natives blended with succulents from South Africa and the Americas, architectural plants originating in New Zealand and the odd South African protea. In a broad sense all have a Gondwanan origin and work particularly well together.

Southern Hemisphere plants also seem to share some interesting characteristics. It may be an ability to withstand hot dry conditions and periodic drought, an adaptation to infertile soil, phosphorous intolerance or similarity of foliage and growth habit. All things considered there is no reason why native plants cannot be integrated into a broader garden composition.

This rooftop space in inner-city Sydney has two separate terraces, one upper and one lower, each with a different character. They face different challenges of wind, rain and sun, but the skill of the designer's planting plan is that both read as one.

In this rooftop garden, space for the garden beds is at a premium. Rainforest species cope well on the shadier, more protected side.

In the more exposed and sunnier beds, a blend of exotic and natives work well. Flannel flowers and kangaroo paws are prominent among the natives.

$\mathcal{T}$he deck above the garage makes an unlikely suntrap for a collection of plants not normally seen together in the wild. However, they blend so seamlessly that it's surprising such combinations have not been tried before.

A Waterwise Native Garden

The owners wanted a garden that used much less water and was predominantly native. The existing garden had overgrown the space and caused damage to the garage below.

The lower section is less exposed and partly shaded, ideal for rainforest plants. The narrow planting bed helps restrict size and the trees planted here grow much like large bonsai. Queensland firewheel tree (*Stenocarpus sinuatus*) and native frangipani (*Hymenosporum flavum*) are the main trees. The lovely wet sclerophyll shrub *Hovea lanceolata* fills in between. The bed is not overplanted. Vireya rhododendrons, *Cordyline fruticosa* 'Rubra' and other groundcover plants such as *Anthurium andreanum* cultivars, mixed bromeliads and the fern *Blechnum brasiliense* fill in the lower levels, especially as the trees grow.

A Way to Mix Natives and Exotics

The idea of mixing natives and exotics is all very well but how do you go about it? Because the two terraces formed two separate microclimates, the solution was to select plants that met the conditions of each one separately.

Planting according to climatic conditions is sensible but rarely done. We tend to want to plant our favourites and then create conditions to make them grow. This is labour intensive and resource heavy. Far better is to analyse the conditions and select plants accordingly. The designer played with the integral qualities of the species to make natives the star performers and backbone planting instead of bit players. While they were growing, exotics and short-term native perennials filled the void and provided floral interest. Principal among them are kangaroo paws in the 'Bush Gem' series and Sydney flannel flowers (*Actinotus helianthi*).

One of the highlights of the garden is the bluish green foliage of kangaroo grass (*Themeda australis* var. 'Mingo'), which hangs over the edge of the border, adding a feathery shawl to the planting. Two unusual grafted grevilleas are *G. alpina*, with small yellow–red flowers, and *G. pimeleoides*, with lovely golden flowers. Rare additions like these give the garden great depth and almost a collector's edge.

A Living Space

The owners use the garden for sitting and dining. A cushion on the long bench downstairs is perfect for catching the morning winter sun. One of the owners works from home and she loves to sit out on winter days and read here. As days get longer a remote-controlled shade canopy covers the space.

As the screen grows on the upper section, greater privacy and more use of this space will follow. At present it is mainly used as a stroll garden, a place to wander and drink in the beauty of the plants. The way the planting has matured is visible in the pictures as the low-level initial planting gives way to a more mature form. The tapestry effect of the succulents, kangaroo paws and flannel flowers will become less important as the grevilleas start to provide colour.

On the lower level, native frangipani (*Hymenosporum flavum*) and Queensland firewheel tree (*Stenocarpus sinuatus*) grow within the raised bed. Both are growing well here and the bed helps constrain growth. Vireya rhododendrons and native *Hovea lanceolata* grow happily with bromeliads such as cultivars of *Guzmania* and *Vriesea* species, *Cordyline fruticosa* and lush fern *Blechnum brasiliense* 'Silver Lady.'

At a Glance	
Complexity	Low
Ability	Professional for hardscaping
Maintenance	Moderate

On the upper level, the true tapestry effect takes hold. Boldly coloured and textured succulents such as black-leafed *Aeonium arboreum* 'Zwartkop' (sometimes sold as 'Schwartzkopf') and silvery *Cotyledon orbiculata* 'Silver Waves'. These form a colour framework along the top bed and other colours and textures were added as contrast and to complement these two. Among them are bloomers like flannel flower and various forms of kangaroo paw (*Anigozanthos* cultivars) for their abundant flowers in white and yellow and red respectively. New Zealand flax and *Cordyline* 'Red Sensation' add reddish highlights and these are picked up with more succulents such as mauve-tinted *Echeveria* 'Afterglow', silvery *Pachyveria* species and golden *Sedum adolphii*.

Tropical Style

The luxuriant growth, perfumes and the vibrant flower colours of tropical gardens appeal to the gardener in all of us. Even if you live in cooler temperate areas, you can still have a garden that looks like a tropical resort. Outside the tropics, it's possible to grow an extraordinary range of plants well outside the normal limits if you have a warm microclimate. It takes some careful consideration of plant material and frost hardiness, but the style is popular from Cairns to Melbourne.

This Sydney garden proves it is possible to defy the odds if the microclimate is right. The owner loved the look of enclosed courtyards and shady verandas common to Balinese and other South-East Asian-style architecture. A central atrium between the rooms that flow into the outdoors provides a protected spot for the garden.

From the street, the garden gate opens to reveal a stand of white bat flower (*Tacca integrifolia*), something of a holy grail for tropical plant enthusiasts. Here they grow en masse, producing up to 40 surreal and strangely beautiful black and white blooms in summer. The flower stems stand about a metre tall against crotons and gingers in the shade of the avocado.

A Lush Look

The owner wanted a garden rich with plants, not a cutting edge designer look. Only four years old, the site had been levelled during construction and only an avocado tree and a frangipani remained. To achieve an established look quickly, advanced trees and shrubs, including several kentia palms and large frangipanis, were craned in. These now form the backbone of the design. Fast-growing subtropical perennials fill out the living tapestry of the new garden.

A Warm Microclimate

Although cold winter winds could damage many tender tropical plants, the central atrium that houses the garden is protected within the enclosing structure of the house. The leafy canopy also protects plants from winter winds. The more tender specimens are cushioned in a blanket of warm air. The balmy warmth lasts right through winter, enabling these rarities not only to survive but also thrive and flower.

Design Elements

Space The garden is actually a series of interconnected court-yards accessed one after the other so that they comprise a series of adventures.

Blending foliage types is one feature of many tropical gardens. So-called tropical or vireya rhododendrons are epiphytic plants and the owner of this garden plants them on the surface of the soil on a mound of coarse orchid compost to improve drainage. Ti plants, blue ginger and young *Licuala ramsayi* surround it.

From the surrounding deck, a lovely rock pool is host to ferns and many exotic orchids. The white flower is Amazon lily (*Eucharis amazonica*).

Mystery and surprise The view through each opening offers enticing glimpses of different floral gems—a mature dragon's blood tree (*Dracaena draco*) in one, giant bromeliads and stands of clumping bamboo in another.

Transition and unity The passage from one courtyard to another gives the viewer a different style of planting to admire. Unity is brought about by keeping each planting style separate.

Plants

Greenhouse beauties like Spanish lady orchids (*Oncidium* species), *Vanda caerulea*, slipper orchids (*Paphiopedilum* species) and the Brazilian orchid *Bifrenaria harrisoniae* need to be positioned in a warm, humid space protected from wind. The latter is found high on cliffs above Rio de Janeiro in Brazil at elevations of 200–800 metres, where you would expect conditions to be cooler than on the beach at Ipanema.

Loose organic matter was added to naturally sandy soil to grow the many semi-epiphytic species that make up the subtropical flora. Epiphytes grow above the surface of the soil, often attached to trees, but are not parasitic. Vireya rhododendrons cope well with root competition provided they have deep organic surface mulch. Flamingo flowers (*Anthurium* species) grow in a rich organic mix lightened with pine bark, while bromeliads respond to orchid bark.

Blue ginger (*Dichorisandra thyrsiflora*) is not a true ginger but one of the tradescantias. It is now seen as one of the best performing subtropicals, with handsome summer foliage and deep blue autumn flowers.

Although cattleyas and orchids are normally hothouse flowers, some are more cool tolerant than others. A specialist orchid nursery should steer you in the right direction. They can be grown in a pot in a warm, well-lit spot in the house, but need a warm, moist microclimate to flower outdoors. A protected outdoor spa often provides this.

Heliconias are the florists' lobster claws and parrot beaks. They won't take frost or cold winds and need a very warm north-facing position protected by walls on the southern side. The easiest to flower in cooler latitudes such as Sydney is *Heliconia latispatha* 'Orange Gyro'. Try also *H. angusta* 'Red Holiday', 'Yellow Holiday' or hybrids 'Hot Rio Nights' or 'Hot Pink'. Most need two summers before they bloom.

Bat plants need warm, filtered sun or dappled shade and a minimum temperature of 15°C. The most common is the

A Balinese-style doorway marks the entrance to the inner courtyard. Indonesian timber sculptures by the door are underplanted with flamingo flowers (*Anthurium* cultivars).

White bat flower (*Tacca integrifolia*). It grows well in pots in warm areas. A drier winter is ideal, as tapering off water in winter is essential. Feed in spring with blood and bone supplemented by regular liquid fertiliser in summer.

Crotons are true tropicals but some large-leafed cultivars can cope with cooler winters. Look for 'Norma', 'Petra', 'Riva' or 'Eura' for protected microclimates or containers.

At a Glance	
Complexity	Moderate
Ability	Design professional
Maintenance	High

Growing Tips

Planting time In a cooler climate, plant subtropical species in late spring when soil has warmed up and growth is active. This allows them a full summer season to establish and gradually acclimatise prior to the onset of colder weather. Do not plant in autumn just before winter sets in.

Microclimates Areas within a garden can vary markedly due to temperature, sun exposure, and moisture. Observe your garden carefully to understand these subtleties; this will help you to select the right plants for each location.

Research No matter where you live, find out as much as you can about tropical plants before you buy. Many thrive in shade but not sun; some will not cope with wind and some prefer slightly drier conditions. Knowledge helps you to select the best spot in your garden for particular plants.

Right: The tropical bat flower (*Tacca integrifolia*) thrives here in the warm humid microclimate, producing dozens of flowers each summer.

Below: A pavilion-style house with a wide veranda surrounds the inner courtyard. The chain in the foreground directs and slows water from the gutter to help refill the pond. Spanish moss (*Tillandsia usneioides*) drapes the frangipani.

International Styles

Water and large stepping stones are a feature of Japanese garden design. Koi carp need a large pond and will destroy most plant life unless it is protected by dividing it from the fish.

Some nations have highly developed garden cultures with instantly recognisable characteristics. European styles include baroque and French provincial, Italian and English gardens. From Asia, those styles most commonly known to us are Japanese, Chinese and Balinese.

If you're attempting to replicate a national look, research it well to achieve genuine integrity. Some of the following examples have been successful largely as a result of the educated use of international garden idioms.

Japanese Gardens

Japanese gardens are spiritual places to a greater or lesser degree. The Zen Buddhist temple gardens of Kyoto, for instance, are filled with symbolic representations of humankind's place in the universe. The two examples shown here represent two distinct strands of garden design in Japan. One adopts a courtyard style; the other is a stroll or landscape garden. Both have certain characteristics in common:

Reverence for nature The natural landscape is idealised and symbolised but never parodied. Because the Japanese landscape is so different to our own and largely unfamiliar, it can be severely misinterpreted by Western gardeners. Garden design is governed by tradition and what occurs in nature. If it doesn't occur in nature, it doesn't fit into the garden. Square ponds, fountains, coloured paving and glass mulches are not part of the tradition. Only in the past decade or so have radical designers veered from the strictures of tradition and added such humanistic elements.

Balance or *sumi* revolves around scale but also the use of objects as representations of natural elements. If these are out of balance the garden will fail in its prime function of providing a refuge from the world. A rock can represent a mountain, pebbles a river or an ocean. There is also an art to their selection: for example, the selected rock should always be in scale. The smaller the garden the more important scale becomes.

Space or *ma* defines the surrounding elements and in turn is defined by them. Empty space and filled space have a synergy in the Japanese garden that is less valued in Western gardens. Like the Chinese yin and yang, it is the attraction of opposites.

Time The Japanese use the term *sabi* to denote time, but it incorporates an additional concept—that of the ideal image of something. Gardeners who appreciate the patina or the aged character of something in a Western garden come close to the meaning of the term. We can understand *sabi* by accepting that a Japanese garden is designed to be beautiful in all seasons, not just autumn or spring. It is common to include elements that shine in each season. The related term *wabi* roughly translates as unique, solitary or one of a kind. *Wabi* is what drives the selection and placement of rocks and the unique designs of individual bonsai.

Right: This hill-and-pond style (*chisen-kaiyu-shiki*) originated in China. Mounds represent hills; a rock represents a mountain outcrop; the overscale lantern represents human presence in the landscape; raked gravel represents a pond or lake. A small space, it is designed to be a viewing garden: the gravel is symbolic; it is not meant to be trampled over, except by the gardener in order to maintain it.

Below: This courtyard garden was designed for the ground-floor apartment in a strata block. The brick fence could not be changed due to body corporate rules, however most Japanese gardens are enclosed. Enclosure is important as in Japan the garden is perceived as a microcosm of nature; the walls, gates and fences serve to isolate it from the world, creating a retreat from the concerns of daily life.

Balinese Gardens

Autralians' love affair with Bali has opened our eyes to the infinite possibilities of Bali's small, enclosed gardens. We love the lushness of Balinese resort gardens, and associate them with relaxing holiday times. But there is also a deeply spiritual side to the island's gardens. Just as the gardens of Japan have their roots in Buddhist thought, so too are Bali's gardens closely associated with Hinduism.

What we know as Balinese style is really a confection devised by Western architects working in Bali. They have embellished local style with colour and broader plant choices to suit resorts and private houses. The true Balinese garden is more ascetic, less flamboyant than we are accustomed to.

Ornamentation to us is often seen as simply an aesthetic element. But Balinese ornaments and features are often shrines, and the Balinese, who see themselves as custodians or caretakers of the land, make offerings daily to the gods. Sandalwood incense is more than just a hippyish exuberance; it is a gesture of thanks. Balinese art is also an expression of this.

Water is an essential element of the modern Balinese garden. Water features may be partially naturalistic, but more often resemble a water tank, rectangular and straight-sided. Carved stone spouts add the rich sound of running water.

The island of Lombok off the southern coast of Bali falls within a different geological area, akin to Darwin, and is generally drier. This can provide a model for drier interpretations of the Bali style in Australia, where water is scarce.

Opposite: The Balinese pavilion has become a popular addition to gardens, particularly if close to a pool. Here, a mix of bougainvillea and colourful cannas give the tropical look in a warm-temperate Sydney garden.

Below: Garden designer Michael White, known as Made Wijaya, is an Australian living and working in South-East Asia. He has been largely responsible for the look we know as 'Balinese'. His own garden on Bali features lush plantings, water gardens and traditional elements such as lanterns and thatched roofs.

A Moroccan lamp hangs from a tree.

Mediterranean Style

Mediterranean gardens are a total experience, mixing architecture that welcomes the outside in with friendly, outdoor spaces adjacent to the house, and plants matched to a generously mild climate.

Mediterranean style is suitable for warm regions everywhere, but it originated in the dry, summer areas around the Mediterranean Sea, where most rain falls in winter, with little or none in summer.

Plants that thrive on minimal water are found commonly in Mediterranean areas and our own natives can often match the look admirably.

Mediterranean features include:

- vibrant, often hot colours, since strong sunlight washes out pastels
- grey foliage, often with heady, aromatic fragrances from essential oils released in summer's heat
- plants such as citrus, conifers and curry bush (*Helichrysum italicum*), lavenders, geraniums, oleanders and perennials for colour
- warm, earthy terracotta in paving or pots
- tiles and mosaic on floors, walls and containers
- pergolas covered with vines such as wisteria or grapes
- geometric design—angular lines and rectangular spaces.

Regional variation is enormous. Gardens we call 'Mediterranean' are often a blend of different styles, each with its own distinct feel and character. Some can be characterised by familiar features, but beware! The elements are derived from centuries of cultural development that is in many ways alien to our own cultural heritage and development. Using themes willy-nilly can lead to a garden mishmash.

Different Mediterranean Styles

Greece Plants are used minimally, either from lack of space, soil or reflected heat. White-painted walls are often covered in bougainvillea or grapevines.

Spain Spanish gardens use formal water features and fountains, often with conifers, roses and fruit trees. Tiles and stuccoed walls are often found.

Provence Pink or earthy tones are signature colours for southern France. Use plants such as lavender, roses, oleanders and perennials.

Tuscany A very controlled and classical Italian style with roots in ancient Greece and Rome. It features formal shapes, statues nestled in niches and parterres, and yellow or ochre lime washes.

North Africa Moorish gardens, the ancestors of the gardens of Spain, are strongly architectural. Tiled courtyards, colonnades and lush plantings give respite from the heat. Moorish gardens are especially apparent in Morocco, though we are possibly more acquainted with the style through its influence over the entire Mediterranean basin rather than from Morocco itself.

Moroccan garden themes have been popular for many years, largely based on the popularity of Moroccan homewares such as tiled wrought-iron tables,

Above left: In an older style apartment building, the gardener, an artist, has used a blend of objects from various Mediterranean countries. In the corner of a garden, the shade of an old tree provides the ideal spot to sit and sip a drink. The turquoise-painted seat looks at home among home-made mosaic plaques.

Above right: Lemons are the quintessential Mediterranean plants.

subtly glazed clay pots and decorative glass lanterns. These alone have led to a garden theme that may not include many of the typical Mediterranean plants. As such they are more an exterior decorating style guaranteed to contribute to outdoor living rather than a specific garden style. But with a little forethought an authentic Moroccan garden can be a useful adjunct to the gardener's arsenal during days of drought and public consciousness about water use.

Plants for Mediterranean Style

Trees

Cypress (*Cupressus sempervirens stricta*)

Judas tree (*Cercis siliquastrum*)

Lotus tree (*Robinia pseudoacacia* 'Frisia')

Peppercorn tree (*Schinus terebinifolia/molle*)

Red-flowering gum (*Corymbia ficifolia*)

Seville orange (*Citrus aurantium*)

Shrubs

Californian tree poppy (*Romneya coulteri*)

Geraldton wax (*Chamaelaucium uncinatum*)

Lavender cotton (*Santolina chamaecyparissus, S. virens*)

Lavender, English (*Lavandula angustifolia*), French (*L. dentata*), Italian (*L. stoechas*)

Rockrose (*Cistus ladanifer, C. salicifolius*)

Groundcovers

Bearded Iris

Catmint (*Nepeta* species)

Convolvulus cneorum

Sea lavender (*Limonium perezii*)

Cherry pie (*Heliotropium arborescens*)

Salvia

Penstemon

Convolvulus sabatius

Curry plant (*Helichrysum italicum*)

Evening primrose (*Oenothera speciosa*)

Perennials

Gaura lindlheimeri cultivars

Russian sage (*Perovskia atriplicifolia*)

Rooftop Bali

This rooftop garden blends the lush resort Bali style with the drier Lombok look. It uses many ornamental features to encapsulate the feel of the Balinese garden but it also contains many interpretations and adaptations.

The garden is atop a four-storey 1970s block of walk-up home units. The outside of the building has been rendered to give its plain brick façade a facelift, and a new structure built on the roof. The building's four wings have been connected with timber boardwalks.

Two separately themed gardens surround the dwelling. One on the south-western side uses Moroccan elements, while this north-eastern garden uses Balinese objects to create a private haven and sanctuary. The gardens are linked by the boardwalks, which give the effect of a garden-in-the-round.

Dealing with a Harsh Environment

Rooftop conditions are notoriously harsh. Wind, cold air, blazing hot sun and a lack of soil and moisture make the lush look hard to achieve naturally. To overcome this, plants are grown in pots and watered with periodic irrigation. Careful plant selection helps plants create their own microclimate most of the time. Tough plants like frangipani, which are succulent in nature, conserve their own moisture and thrive in the harsh, sunny conditions. Water in large pots helps create humidity.

An apartment constructed on the roof of a 1970s unit block is the unlikely setting for a feast of Balinese objects. Everything is grown in pots but they are cleverly disguised and even the paving can be lifted and moved if need be.

The Balinese habit of using the outdoors for eating, relaxing and socialising
is reflected in the long, rustic timber
table surrounded by Balinese and other
compatible decorative objects.

Design Elements

Mystery Authentic Balinese temple doors open to reveal a large daybed in one corner. This section is not visible until the doors are opened; you can then step through the narrow, shallow but ornate doorway typical of Balinese dwellings. This act of stepping up and bending down seems to encourage a spiritual element into our appreciation of the style.

Focal points include the daybed, the richly carved and painted doors (when closed), the crocodile bench and the timber dining table.

Space The area is divided into separate rooms and functions. Functionally, outdoor spaces are closely linked to the relevant interior spaces. The outdoor dining space is directly off the residence and near to the kitchen. Barbecue facilities are located on the side, with window access to the kitchen. After dinner, guests can retire to the outdoor lounging area through the decorative gates, or to the interior, depending on the weather. Both areas have a clear view of proceedings on the rest of the roof, but are distinct and separate.

Materials Flooring includes recycled materials such as hardwood sleepers, old weathered bricks and sandstone off-cuts. Wherever they are used, blue-green rumbled pebbles work as a unifying element.

On rooftops, drainage can be a major problem and the cost of removing fixed paving is prohibitive should the protective membrane need checking or repair. Because of this, permanent materials were not used; all flooring surfaces can be removed or replaced if the need arises.

Structure Engineered to high standards and to withstand severe windstorms, there is a high level of safety. Objects needed to be weighted down or fixed in place in case of storms.

Unity comes from the use of consistent materials in both plant life and in containers, which are mostly terracotta with red Balinese bricks.

Boundaries The walls of the roof are thickly planted and edged with a timber surround for consistency.

Texture Pebbles, timber, stone and plant forms contribute to a richly textured garden. Leaf shape, form and colour all contribute to the overlaying depth.

Stone elephants and a carved water bowl are given an air of permanence by enclosing pebbles in an old rope barrier.

Plants

A range of tough subtropicals give a lush look and
are durable in the conditions:

Philodendron 'Xanadu'

Cast iron plant (*Aspidistra elatior*)

Cycas revoluta

Bromeliads

Dianella ensifolia 'Border Silver'

Mondo grass

Rhapis palm

Strelitzia nicolae

Ctenanthe species.

From inside the living room, the main focal point is a long, carved crocodile bench that stands sentinel over the main terrace view. A collection of
artefacts give the sitting area an authentic air.

Blue Moroccan Garden

This Melbourne garden uses olives and other dry-climate plants around a paved courtyard designed for year-round use. A pond and stepped-down area come directly off the back of the house and offer a passage to the terrace, which is the heart of the design. Locating this away from the house ensures maximum sun and prevents long shadows imposing on the owners' enjoyment of this sunny space. An area of lawn lined with shrubs planted for privacy fills the back section, leading to a garage with rear lane access.

The seating area has the feel of a sunken pit, an effect created by surrounding the space with low walls. The floor is Indian slate paving with tile highlights. High walls common to many Moroccan houses are softened by potted shrubs and trees along the perimeters.

Making the Most of the Outdoors

In a cooler climate, outdoor living possibilities are fewer than in a milder climate but there are ways to maximise warmth and the potential to enjoy the outdoors in many seasons.

Lush foliage is less desirable in winter and the absence of large trees, except as perimeter plantings, means that there are no cold shadows. The courtyard is sunny and bright on warmer winter days, so the space is well used by the family.

A Place for Entertaining

Bringing furniture inside in bad weather is a time-consuming business, as is the process of assembling it when a party is in the offing. A large paved terrace with built-in seating provides a focal point for outdoor living. All-weather cushions covered with UV-stabilised fabric assure comfort and can be stored indoors to extend their life. Packing and storing cushions is easier than folding and lugging timber seats around. The benches are also useful for putting drinks down on.

There is room for large gatherings to meet and feel comfortable around the outdoor fireplace. Portable outdoor gas space heaters could be added for short-term heat if required.

Design Elements

Space The garden is strongly directional. A path takes a straight line through to the end without the need to meander through plants or seating. This keeps the seating area out of the main traffic line, creating a rest zone. The low masonry walls give the feel of a conversation 'pit' without it being in any sense a sunken garden.

Structure Indian slate paving forms the central structural element, with tile highlights.

Boundaries High walls common to many Moroccan houses are softened by potted shrubs and trees along the perimeters.

Matching the Garden with the House

The garden needed to fit in with the architecture of the house, which was not necessarily Moroccan in theme. The walls of the house were rendered and painted in the same colour as the garden walls, and they simply disappear. The warm colours give the garden an authentic feel. Attention is directed to the garden by the placement of walls, ponds and hedges.

A contemporary renovation gave the owners of this space a chance to indulge their love of all things Moroccan. The neighbour's walls were painted pale terracotta and a false wall with numerous niches set the scene with mood lighting and earthy-coloured, textured ornaments.

A French Provincial Garden

This low-maintenance garden functions as an outdoor room in both winter and summer, bringing a touch of Gallic charm to a crowded inner-city precinct. Its inspiration is French provincial and it certainly has the feel of a village square in Provence, surrounded by buildings, brick and stone, warm with the patina of age. On the ground, crushed gravel scrunches underfoot as you head for the quaintly antique café chairs; it also forms a natural petanque or bocce court, popular with guests.

Two wrought-iron gates form the main focal point for this 'village square'. They provide a backdrop to the original 1830s house. Even though they are very much English colonial, they enhance the garden's Gallic charm. Similar gates are usually painted so thickly that all detail is lost, but leaving them to oxidise naturally adds to the effect.

Making the Garden Shapes Work

The garden is roughly rectangular but with an L-shaped configuration and odd-shaped annexes. These had to be integrated into the garden as a whole.

The garden is about 9 metres wide. At one end, it measures only 3 metres but expands to 6 metres opposite where it abuts the gates. The solution was to create a separate service area housing wheelie bins and rear access in the annexes. The antique gates separate the two areas. From the garden, the view through the grille is of a classic wall fountain in a chic French style surrounded by creeping fig.

Going for Low Maintenance

The owner is often away and the space had to care for itself. A spare modernist styling did not suit the owner who had many older pieces of furniture brought from previous houses.

The gravel acts as a rain soak and an earthy connection with the transposed French provincial feel. It is not completely maintenance-free. Leaves need to be raked regularly, and sweeping or raking cleans up most weeds. The citrus are easily fed four times a year by scattering fertiliser around the drip line and watering it in or waiting for the rain. The wisteria is able to thrive on nutrients in the soil. There are no beds to dig.

Fitting the Garden to the House

The period nature of the building dating from the 1830s had to be preserved and the garden had to fit with it. The colonial era brick cottage has a warm, aged quality, which is reflected also in the garden's decomposed granite surface. The simple lines of the building are repeated in the spare and simple design of the garden. The effect is enhanced by the inclusion of elements redolent of French country style without the usual gimmickry associated with 'Mediterranean-style' gardens. Authenticity comes from the architecture around the garden and the openness of the setting.

The simplicity of a French country village square was the inspiration for this low-maintenance garden that defies convention by eschewing both grass and paving, opting instead for decomposed granite. It is serviceable and largely carefree—plus it doubles as a boules court when guests are around. The simple, formal planting is restricted to potted clipped figs, wisteria, climbing roses and the large citrus trees.

Design Elements

Scale Two oversized bay trees in terracotta containers give the illusion of a larger space and give the garden drama and impact.

Plants

There are two dominant trees: an existing mandarin in the centre of the courtyard and a tuckeroo beyond the wall. Citrus are popular plants in southern France and add a true Côte d'Azur feel. The mandarin and another existing plant, a cumquat, are a natural fit. The canopy of the mandarin was raised by trimming and opening up the trunk line to form a small tree. The decomposed granite comes right to the trunk. It needs feeding four times a year with citrus food applied out to the dripline at the end of the leaf canopy.

Tuckeroo (*Cupaniopsis anacardioides*) is a native coastal tree growing to 10 metres, but usually smaller. It has yellow berries and large, attractive leathery leaves.

Chinese star jasmine (*Trachelospermum chinensis*) grows anywhere, anyhow. Use it as a hedge, a wall plant or even a groundcover. Train it as topiary or a shrub. It is tough and

An alcove of the main courtyard is reserved for a small vegetable garden and service bins. However, all the viewer sees through the antique gate is this charming wall fountain.

The old Victorian gate and its rather grand gateposts are left unpainted and the rust effect adds to the authenticity.

forgiving. Three star jasmines replaced some failing roses. (One survives, a rambler 'Cecile Brunner', on the boundary fence retained as living barbed wire.)

Three wisterias on the adjacent wall shade a rooftop garden on the first floor. Wisteria is the classic two-week wonder but what a fortnight! It needs a strong framework if grown over a trellis but here it is trained up the wall on a single stem and grown sparsely from there.

Bay (*Laurus nobilis*) is a culinary plant and responds well to topiary. It tolerates drought and is ideal for containers.

How To Do It

Decomposed granite Lay decomposed granite on a compacted stratum of granite rammed with a machine called a vibrating or compacting plate, commonly known as a whacker. This creates a solid but porous surface. (Hire companies have them if you feel like doing it yourself.) Mix quartz sand with the second layer of granite and add white cement for a firmer, more permanent surface.

Several authentic French café tables, available from antique stores, are dotted around the space and make a far less imposing footprint on the space than a full-sized outdoor dining setting. Three star jasmines growing on wires attached to the wall will eventually form columns up the entire height of the building to soften the brickwork.

A few potted geraniums add colour near the back door.

At a Glance

Complexity Low

Ability Amateur or professional elements

Maintenance Low

Santa Fe Garden

Santa Fe style is a product of the fusion of native American materials with the architectural heritage of Spain. The original residents of the south-western United States, the Anasazi, employed adobe—sun-dried clay bricks mixed with grasses for strength, mortared with simple mud, and then covered with additional protective layers of mud—for shelters. While it is essentially an architectural style, in the garden its main characteristics are the use of built elements with waterwise plants.

True Santa Fe style is a product of its climate—high mountain plains with cold, snowy winters and hot, dry summers. In this Sydney garden, the designer has interpreted the style to suit the site. Reusing naturally weathered materials was an inspired choice that lends an air of authenticity.

A rustic deck of recycled timber surrounds the house. An old garage was rendered and painted in limewash to simulate the look of faded paint, while new brick or besser block walls divide up spaces and create interesting glimpses into other outdoor rooms.

Left: Old timber beams and recycled iron lace panels finished in a rust colour are combined with traditional red desert colours. The iron lace panels give an impression of old Spanish grilles, enhancing the theme.

Materials

Create the look of antiquity with weathered timbers. These are becoming scarcer these days but timber merchants may have old pier timbers or building supports. Some garden designers also have a stock of such materials and use them in their designs. Ask representatives of the Australian Institute of Landscape Designers and Managers (AILDM) in your state for possible sources. Contact http://www.aildm.com.au

Think of creative ways of using ornamental elements to convey a theme. For instance, iron lace is adaptable and can give a hint of another culture without the need for expensive authentic pieces. Here it gave a Spanish look but it could easily have worked also in an Indian theme.

Plants

Plants are a combination of succulents and east coast rainforest, an unlikely mix but here used skilfully. *Agave attenuata* is a commonly grown succulent that adapts to many climates. The soil in this garden is a poor sandy loam laid over a sandstone outcrop so it drains quickly, providing a good growing medium for succulents.

At a Glance

Complexity Moderate

Ability Design professional for construction

Maintenance Low

Extreme *Spaces*

Just as there are extreme sports fanatics, there are mad keen gardeners who seek to establish a garden regardless of the conditions—albeit with considerably less risk to life and limb. It happens all over the world. In crowded Tokyo, enterprising gardeners attach frames to their roofs with access by ladder from their narrow 1 metre balcony. Here, they tend bonsai trees to perfection. In Spain, villagers adorn walls with terracotta pots filled with geraniums. Swiss alpine sheds are adorned with houseleeks, the lovely sempervivums that thrive on rooftops.

Solving the Problem Sites

There is always room for a garden, but small spaces do present some acute design issues that must be addressed. Some sites challenge the very presence of a garden. The space may be a tiny light well, shaded for most of the day except when the summer sun is at its highest. A garden on top of a building will be buffeted by winds and scorched by sun. A space may be so tiny that there is barely room for the gardener to turn around. The slope of the garden may defy the gardener's will; soil in such a location is usually thin and poor, leached and washed away by rain.

Where space is tight, use climbers on walls to create a vertical garden. This creeping fig is tightly clipped.

Shade and Sun

Small gardens are often alternately in full sun or full shade, making plant selection difficult. Both sun- and shade-loving plants are generally happy to live in areas of dappled light—sunlight may be filtered through leafy natural canopy or a constructed shade canopy such as a lattice, lathe or a slatted framework. But plants find it difficult to adjust to exposure to intense midday sun, followed by many hours of heavy shade, a common phenomenon in confined spaces with high walls and adjacent buildings. Deep shadows from buildings or walls may limit what grows without blemish—and blemishes are magnified in a small space.

In winter, sun-loving plants may only get two or three hours' sun per day, often insufficient for them to thrive. In summer, shade-loving plants have the opposite problem. Intense sun during the hottest part of the day can scorch the leaves, leaving them looking dishevelled at a time when we are most likely to spend time in our outdoor living space.

Careful plant selection can solve these problems, but it's important to wait until the main design ideas are formulated before planting.

Many Needs, Little Space, Odd Shapes

It's hard to satisfy multiple needs and desires—for example the need for access and privacy, a desire for lavish plantings and to enjoy outdoor living—when there is barely room to satisfy one function. And how do you create views or points of interest in a garden totally enclosed by high walls or buildings? Focal points such as wall fountains or statuary, plant sculpture, topiary, bonsai, espalier and specimen potted plants are all ways to do this.

These pages show several views of a roof garden within a redeveloped factory building converted to apartments. The garden fits within an area formerly part of the fabric of the building but opened up to provide an outdoor living space. Facing west, it is partially shaded by two large broad-leafed tea trees (*Melaleuca quinquenervia*) on the street. The height of the walls causes some shading problems, especially in the morning when the eastern sun is blocked by the building. In winter the effect is more problematic. In summer, heavy shade is followed by full afternoon sun. Plants that could cope with both extremes were selected.

Right A boar's head fountain gives the space a formal Mediterranean feel.

These issues are also common in larger gardens, but in a small space they are magnified and concentrated. You simply cannot move the compost heap or plant a tree somewhere else.

Sometimes outdoor living space has to be sacrificed in difficult terrain. It is hard, for instance to introduce an alfresco ambience on a steep slope or indeed to set up table and chairs in a narrow light well between two high buildings. You may need to take a different approach, for example making the plants the major attraction of a garden.

Many small gardens have odd corners, narrow passages and tiny courtyards that can be hard to deal with in a coherent way. They are slotted in to asymmetrical plots demanded by the pressures of building or extensions to a dwelling. Dealing with these problems requires a few useful techniques.

Techniques for Dealing with Odd Spaces

Plant lovers often create a 'stroll' garden, building a path that wends its way through a collection of plants. Even in a very small or oddly shaped garden, you may find room to create some sort of path, even if its very short. Some of our examples fit that mould. Others use the space as a visual feast, something to savour or to indulge themselves in their passion for gardening in its own right.

The biggest problem facing designers or homeowners is how to come up with a design that looks balanced or unified. One way is to re-orient your sight lines. Controlling where the eye goes is the key. For example, if your unadorned or unimproved space looks straight out onto a car park or some other unattractive object, use a bank of plants, or a wall or trellis, to hide it.

In a narrow garden, make paths for the eye to follow. They create a line of sight. Curving or diagonal paths can suggest the end of a garden is around the corner, giving the illusion of a larger space.

Narrow gardens can also be divided into 'rooms' to enhance the sense of space. To create rooms, screen off areas with lattice, walls, fences, bamboo or other plants to make a narrow entrance or doorway into the next section. Have a path leading between sections, with turns of up to 90 degrees that force a new perspective on the viewer.

To make a shallow garden seem deeper, have a pathway zigzag around obstructions, making the route through the garden longer and more indirect. Use plantings such as a tree, a low hedge or a screen of shrubs to break up the space.

To create more mystery in a square-shaped garden, divide the area into formal geometric spaces.

Opposite: A tiny light well in a townhouse is filled with shade-loving palms, ferns and subtropical plants that cope with the low light. It acts as a visual treat and a lung for the interior living room that looks into it.

Below: The entrance way to this tiny Victorian semi-detached house is filled with large containers of rare exotics while the row of Buddhist prayer napkins hide the neighbouring house.

A Light-well Garden

Sydney's Kings Cross is not an area known for its gardens. This tiny garden is crammed into the narrow space between two four-storey apartment blocks.

This is the extreme plantsman's courtyard, a garden space confined on at least three sides and epitomising the problems of small inner-city gardens. Planners never envisaged a garden in a space like this. They may have assumed that occupants of the ground-floor flats would dot a few pot plants around the door and that perhaps a window box would adorn upper storeys, but here the concreted space is entirely devoted to growing in containers.

The plants have been chosen for their resilience—a case of trial and error—and for their viewing value from the upper floors of the two buildings. Only the ground-floor occupants have an eye-level view. Cane-stemmed plants with fan- or umbrella-like leaves look good from above. This is the strength of the garden. Tolerance of shade is the other determinant. Plants of subtropical or rainforest origins most frequently share these characteristics.

In summer, some parts of the area get a full blast of sun for a short period of the day, and up to two hours in high summer. This pierces through a 1.3-metre gap in the buildings. When it passes, the plants are cast into full shade for the rest of the day. In winter, it gets no sun at all. So in summer plants normally in shade receive scorching direct sun at midday when the sun is at its hottest. It is particularly difficult if temperatures rise into the high 30–40°C range. Cushioned by a microclimate, many of the plants are able to sail through all but the hottest days without blemish.

Creating a Warm Microclimate

The owner has carefully chosen plants that can survive the colder conditions and lack of sun, but they do so because they form a plant community, which in turn creates a protective microclimate—a cushion of warm air protects more tender plants. Fortunately, frost is not an issue here—the buildings prevent cold air from settling and eddies from the northern side of the building keep air circulating.

Lessons from Nature

In every respect, the space between the two buildings resembles that between tall cliff faces. It is an urban canyon and it is to natural mountain chasms that we should look for solutions. In nature, every nook and cranny is colonised by a specially adapted plant community. The key to working with difficult spaces is to choose those plants that originate in similar situations. Plants that grow at the base of enclosing cliffs are usually adapted to dank, damp, shady conditions. And even tropical and subtropical plants may encounter short periods of extreme cold. In fact, in many tropical mountain regions, where many of our houseplants originated, near-zero temperatures may occur for a short period overnight—the canopy protects leaves from frost. In the garden, a tree or other overhead protection can prevent frost from forming in areas where temperatures regularly drop to zero. A similar situation protects plants in this garden.

Growing in Containers

The major difficulty of growing in pots is the risk of drying out. This is reduced when plants are massed, as they are here, as the microclimate reduces evaporation and keeps humidity around the foliage. Watering is not often required, except in hot, dry conditions. This part of the east coast has a relatively dry winter and winter watering may be required, particularly as the temperatures rise in August.

From the top floors of the two 1920s apartment buildings, the dramatic impact of large subtropical plants is revealed.

Variegated foliage lifts the gloom of the space and makes it seem bright and inviting. Campelia is the dominant plant but Chinese happy plant and dumb cane (or dieffenbachia) also add their white or cream flecks.

The biggest problem here is dampness. Although water drains away, it can stay moist around the roots and stems. Allowing the soil in the containers to dry out is often the only way to maintain vigour. In this inner-city location, dust settles on leaves and can clog the pores, preventing them breathing properly, so leaves need to be hosed clean. The skill of the gardener comes from knowing just how wet plants need to be in different seasons.

Competition from root growth could be a problem in restricted soil conditions, say, in a garden bed. But containers can be lifted and plants repotted, divided or root pruned. Each plant grows in its own restricted space without hindrance from more-aggressive neighbours.

Plants

Variegated cultivars of dieffenbachia and cane-stemmed begonias were the first plants to begin the experiment. These were followed by syngoniums, spathiphyllums, dracaenas and blue ginger (*Dichorisandra thyrsiflora*) most of which have darkish, broad green leaves.

Campelia (*Tradescantia zanonia*), rare in cultivation, brings light into the space. It has the same broad fan arrangement of leaves and cane-stems as blue ginger, but the foliage is white, splashed with green stripes. Small, insignificant cream–white flowers resemble the common tradescantia flower found in smaller tradescantia species such as wandering jew.

By blending ferns, palms and climbing plants like hoyas, which have been trained on wires across the light well, and syngoniums, which attach themselves to the walls and downpipes, the garden is allowed to grow vertically up out of the cavernous space. Taller plants like Chinese happy plant (*Dracaena fragrans* 'Massangeana') fit into corners, growing to first-floor height in order to reach the light. Many rainforest shrubs such as Macleay laurel (*Anopterus macleayanus*) will also adapt to this type of space.

Many plants in this garden are rare in cultivation, sourced or bred by the owner himself. For example, Queen Emma lily (*Crinum angustum*) may not be available. Try other crinums, including the summer-flowering pink hybrid *C.* x *powellii* and the fragrant native swamp lily (*C. pedunculatum*), which flowers in spring.

Angel's trumpets (*Brugmansia* x *candida*) flower in soft gelato colours like apricot, white, pink and lemon. They perfume the garden at dawn and dusk. As they are easy to grow from cuttings, dispose of prunings carefully.

Some gingers are cold sensitive, such as many in the *Costus* genus. Others, such as hardy native ginger (*Zingiber caerulea*) or orange ginger (*Hedychium greenei*), will adapt to the conditions in this type of space. *Costus pictus* 'Pink Sphere' survives here despite its being cold sensitive in Sydney.

Blue ginger (*Dichorisandra thyrsiflora*) is a herbaceous perennial that may die back in cooler winter gardens. It regrows as soil warms in spring. The unusual two-toned blue-on-blue flowers appear in autumn. Grown in the ground they form a decent-sized clump with many stems and flower heads; they need a wide deep pot, as the roots form large storage vessels that look like dahlia tubers.

Purple or white *Globba winitii* 'Thai Beauty' is a dwarf ginger for pots or shady beds. Tulip gingers (*Curcuma* species), so named for the shape of their flowering spikes, have names like 'Siam Sweetheart' or 'Jewel of Thailand'. They prefer shade, summer humidity and moisture. Keep the tubers dry in winter by storing the pot on its side out of the weather.

Hoyas or wax flowers are climbing plants. Their fragrant clustered flowers form year after year on the same flower stalk. Unusual ones growing here include pink-and-white-flowered *Hoya shepherdii* and the brick red *H. pubicalyx*.

The orchid *Stanhopea tigrina* flowers from the base and is suited to basket planting.

This close up of the flowers of campelia show it to be a relative of the common tradescantia known as wandering jew or creeping jesus.

Subtropical Plant Tips

To get the best results with little care or attention, subtropical plants prefer:

- a warm, frost-free microclimate
- plentiful natural rainfall
- moist summers
- protection from drying northerly summer winds and winter westerlies.

At a Glance

Complexity Moderate

Ability Design professional for construction

Maintenance Low

A Modern Sloping Garden

S loping sites can pose many problems, and gardening on a slope can be hard work. Gardens tend to follow gravity after heavy rain or when soil dries out, and slippage can be a serious issue.

The main feature of this garden is a large and majestic Sydney red gum or smooth-barked apple (*Angophora costata*). Although this species dominates the wooded slopes of Sydney Harbour, it has suffered from encroachment and is rarely replanted. This tree became the focus of the design and the garden's inspiration.

Preserving a Tree

With the decision to make the angophora the inspiration for the garden it had to be preserved. However, building and constructing around trees is a tricky business especially with those as sensitive as angophora.

The site's 45 degree incline required terracing and retaining walls. Fortunately, the new garden conformed to the existing levels and further excavation was minimised. Angophoras don't like root disturbance but the tree's natural habit protected it. The roots of the angophora grow under and between the rock formation and sometimes the roots spread a buttress-like shawl over rocky outcrops. Excavation was minimised to prevent disturbing the roots and rock. Here a sandstone ledge protected the tree.

Ensuring Privacy

In this front garden, passers-by had a dress circle view into the garden so finding a means to ensure privacy was the first dilemma to solve. Putting in a high fence was ruled out by council regulations but planting solved the problem. An informal hedge of lillypilly (*Acmena smithii* var. *minor*) provides a dense but friendly screen, more amenable to the streetscape than a wall but still solid enough to defeat the auditorium feel.

Retaining Soil

Steep slopes are hard to plant as soil tends to follow gravity. In the bush, natural rock outcrops hold back soil, but in suburbia most of the great outcrops disappear during building so artificial means become necessary. Retaining walls across the breadth of the garden provide generous planting pockets and suggested a layered planting scheme. The walls were constructed of dry-packed golden sandstone, providing a visual link with the original sandstone of the foreshore slopes.

*S*andstone and a mix of architectural and foliage plants enhance this sunken courtyard.

Controlling Tannin Stains

The leaves of the angophora, and indeed all gums, produce tannin. Tannin stains paving, especially when wet, but it can be controlled. Sweep up regularly before the tannins have a chance to leach out. A carefully applied wash of weak muriatic acid can clear stains. Muriatic acid is weak solution of sulphuric acid and burns skin, so make sure you wear protective clothing if doing the job yourself. It is sold in hardware stores for cleaning bricks, and regularly applied by bricklayers at the end of a job. If you prefer a more natural solution, strong sunlight and time helps bleach the worst effects.

Design Elements

Space The stepped nature of the design makes the space look bigger through a series of transitions demanded by the site. The large (50 x 50 centimetres) blue–grey Riverstone concrete pavers also help a small space appear larger.

Focal point The finishing touch is a striking water feature carved from a block of granite. Its shape—a circular step pyramid, almost Mesopotamian inspired—is certainly

eye-catching and suits the position, viewed as it is either from the stairs above or at eye level from the front door.

Colours are subdued to go with the plant palette. Aubergine, grey and a deep aquamarine on the garage wall were chosen to complement the foliage. The dark colour of the paving is less glary on sunny days and complements the plantings. The muted colours work well together with the contrasting blue–grey wall on the steps.

Plants

This garden relies almost entirely on foliage for its colour. Flowers are few although the angophora puts on a generous display of white blossom in November. The layers of plants work as bands of colour accented by vertical foliage plants including purple Moses in a basket (*Tradescantia pallida* 'Purple Heart') and *Rhoeo spathacea*. There are plum, purple, white-variegated and silver plants interspersed with banks of many different greens.

Cordyline 'Red Sensation' is a recent introduction, adding plum highlights to the green of *Liriope muscari* 'Evergreen Giant' and *Cycas revoluta*. A line of foxtail grass (*Pennisetum alopecuroides*) softens the top run of plants, providing a further strip of green, almost chartreuse, as contrast to the red cordy-

lines and the narrower *Cordyline nigra*, another species of *Cordyline* with an upright habit and black-tinged foliage.

Adding a touch of white to these darker tonings is *Dianella ensifolia* 'Border Silver'. A newer addition is cushion bush (*Leucophyta brownii* 'Silver Nugget'), a native coastal plant with silvery leaves that always looks as if the light has been left on. A row of them is planted at the edge of the path. Silver leaves have the uncanny knack of reflecting light day and night and are ideal to use where you may want to highlight an edge or border.

Above: Beautifully interlocking sandstone blocks show the warmth of the indigenous stone outcrops and tie the garden to its setting.

Opposite top: A spiral granite fountain is the centrepiece of the courtyard.

Opposite bottom: From the paved area the garden rises steeply to street level. The tiered plantings were designed around a magnificent Sydney red gum (*Angophora costata*).

Very Small Spaces

Very small gardens demand creative solutions to the space deficit. Passageway gardens in particular are daunting. Their success depends very much on how the boundaries and ground surfaces are prepared.

Garden 1: A Narrow Courtyard Garden

The owner of this narrow garden has treated it as a changing stage set. It is small enough to regularly change the decorative elements and plantings to suit his mood or satisfy his craving for a gardening experience when there is little room.

A large sliding steel-framed door completely opens the inside to the outside, increasing the perception of size. The original configuration of the house, built in 1894, was a doglegged double L-shape. The rear service section, including bathroom and kitchen, was completely remodelled to create a wider, regularly shaped rectangle.

Creating Privacy

The garden is sandwiched between two terrace houses in the inner city and lacked privacy. This was addressed by increasing the apparent height of the fence by about 35 centimetres with a false pergola frame. Vines grown along wires strung between the support posts now completely hide the neighbour's unrenovated roofline. These have grown sufficiently dense to be trimmed and maintained as an attractive, impenetrable hedge.

Flooring Solutions

The interior tiles are polished concrete, mirrored by Haddonstone concrete pavers outside. The convergence of materials helps to unify the two spaces. Polished black pebbles are set into the 5 millimetre gap between the pavers to define the linear perspective. Originally, mini mondo grass was planted between each but as this is both an outdoor living area with seating and a passageway it was impractical. The mondo wore out from frequent footfall and chairs wedged themselves in the soft edges, making sitting uncomfortable.

Using a Narrow Space

A large teak bench, which seems out of scale for the site, is however frequently used for reading, lounging and conversation. Restricting planting to large containers frees up the fence space, giving a view back into the house and garden. Less roomy seating previously in place was not used nearly as often, so there is some method to the madness of scaling up.

Plants

A tropical theme is evident in the planting that changes with the season. Between the star jasmine (*Trachelospermum jasminoides*), the owner has planted a few other vines for seasonal variety. A Carolina jessamine (*Gelsemium sempervirens*) adds its sweet baby powder fragrance and yellow flowers in autumn and winter. Climbing frangipani (*Chonemorpha fragrans*), a tropical vine not often grown in the Sydney climate, fills in after the star jasmine in summer. This is a vigorous climber that loves the heat and once it gets its head in the sun it never looks back. The perfume is identical to the common frangipani, heady and persistent, with the flowers typical of the whorled shape of blooms in the Apocynaceae family that includes oleanders, star jasmine, *Mandevilla* and *Plumeria*. It needs several years to reach flowering stage but then each year it increases its production of flowers and can become a display every bit as dramatic as *Mandevilla* 'White Fantasy'—with perfume.

Brugmansias are grown from large 1-metre cuttings and regularly replaced as they outgrow the space. In summer, they root rapidly and start producing flowers in six to ten weeks.

Little more than the width of a path—three concrete pavers wide—this garden is a tiny retreat with a tropically themed planting.

Garden 2: A Passageway garden

Older style apartments never had provision for gardens. The prevailing idea in the 1940s and 1950s when they were built was that these were dormitory buildings for single people or shift workers who would not be interested in gardening.

Nevertheless, the owner of this garden, which is no more than a passageway to the front entrance, has turned it into a subtropical oasis using containers.

Planting for the Position

The garden faces west, but a high wall shades it in the afternoon. Reflected light hits the white-painted wall and helps warm the plants without overheating them. Again it's a case of using the microclimate to best advantage. Some taller shrubs planted in the ground hug the wall and provide shade for the begonias, justicias and other soft-stemmed subtropical perennials that dominate the planting. Most of the plants chosen prefer a semi-shaded position. Without the wall and shrubs, this garden could have been a hotbox and the choice of plants would have been much different. Mediterranean perennials and succulents may have then been more suitable.

Feeding Plants with Worm Castings

Each plant is grown to perfection using a standard potting mix and regular applications of an excellent liquid manure made from the drainings from the worm farm. Worm-casting liquid is very strong and can burn the roots and leaves of plants, so must be diluted in a ratio of one part worm liquid to four parts water. If in doubt, make the solution to the colour of weak tea.

The castings themselves are less potent after rain. Remove all worms before adding the castings to containers as a compost or mulch. Worms in pots can lead to leaching of soil, and their tunnels can leave the way open for ants, mealy bugs and other undesirable pests.

Grown entirely in pots, magnificent tree begonias and justicias are fed regularly to maintain such vigour. These plants flower from spring to autumn. Many begonias languish when grown in the ground, usually due to root competition. Growing them in pots resolves this problem.

Odd-shaped Spaces

Once the children have grown up and moved out of the family home, mature couples often find that caring for a large yard and a sprawling house eats into newfound leisure time. The issue is not gardening but rather the constant mowing and high maintenance involved in tending a large garden. Is this really what life is all about?

One solution combines the advantages of villa living with the security of full Torrens Title. These compact but spacious townhouses are located in an 'over fifties' community and each has its own garden.

The houses open onto a paved courtyard area with a pergola attached. The design of each garden is left to individual owners so some may have a patch of lawn while others opt for paving, gravel or planting beds.

Both gardens described here fit onto oddly shaped blocks. Measured at the widest point, they average approximately 12 x 4 metres—not a big space but enough to develop an interesting, even captivating, small garden. A narrow service area on one side measures about 3 x 10 metres.

Each townhouse has a small front garden, a side garden where the utilities—clothesline, water heater and so on—are located and a bigger space on the opposite side which is viewed from the interior living areas.

Improving the Soil

After building was completed, the developers installed a one-size-fits-all garden. It's cheap, it's tough and it's just like every other garden. The biggest challenge for the new owners was the soil. Like many housing estates, the topsoil had been scraped off, leaving a wasteland of hard-packed clay. A thin veneer of topsoil, enough to establish a lawn but insufficient to promote good growth, was returned but serious soil amendment was necessary. Soil is the key to gardening. Take time to fix it and you won't be disappointed. Truckloads of clay were removed and replaced with quality topsoil and compost to form a good planting base.

A Difficult Aspect

The gardens are located at the top of a south-west-facing valley. The ground was fast draining and the westerly sun desiccating. Tough plants were chosen to ensure they would survive and thrive.

A zigzagging path leads from the side passage to the garden at the rear.

Garden 1

Outdoor living is the key to the design of this space. The owners are active seniors with a busy social life. They wanted a place in which to relax and entertain. The ground space was narrow and overlooked by a neighbouring building. They opted for large clay 30 x 30 centimetre pavers. The larger the paver, the less busy a space appears and this was important in such a small space. At the end of the long view of the side yard a cleverly placed water feature acts as a focal point. This also distracts attention from the wall and the fence above it.

A zigzag box hedge directs our eye along the line so it seems wider and takes attention from the inward angled retaining wall. The shaping of the hedge encourages the eye to dart from side to side and the design principle of apparent movement increases our perception of space.

Plants

Easy-care plants like lilyturf *Liriope muscari* 'Evergreen Giant', dark-leafed cordylines, massed *Pennisetum* grasses and *Canna* 'Tropicanna' give a structured feel to the front garden. Box (*Buxus microphylla* var. *japonica*) is one of the most versatile of all the box cultivars. *Gardenia* 'Florida' grows to about a metre and is the most free flowering in a frost-free garden out of the tropics. Variegated sweet flag (*Acorus gramineus* 'Ogon') tolerates both dry and damp spots and adds foliage texture and colour. Purple lily turf (*Liriope muscari* 'Evergreen Giant') is a tough customer with attractive spikes of purple flowers in autumn. Bird of paradise flower (*Strelitzia reginae*) loves hot, dry conditions with an occasional drenching. It flowers from autumn to spring.

*T*he front of the small townhouses has been carefully planted with grasses, kingfisher daisies and agaves to reduce maintenance and watering requirements.

Small Space Tips

Plant height Keeping plants low focuses our attention down and along the line of the garden. Large or bulky plants could appear overwhelming and shrink the available space.

Garden 2

This small garden courtyard is a haven of soft mauves and silver foliage. Lawn was retained as a backdrop to the foliage, flower and painted surfaces. These are all in muted greys and purples with a dash of cream and white.

Colours and Architectural Shapes

The owner's favourite flower colours are purple and mauve and a silver foliage theme complements them. The building is painted in shades of soft grey, purple, aubergine and pumpernickel. These blend well with the foliage colours without making any outrageous look-at-me statement.

The choice of plants adds a succession of seasonal colour. Furry-leafed lamb's ears bloom in late spring but the leaves look strong and appealing year-round. The vanilla scent of cherry pie or heliotrope dominates from summer until autumn, when an edging of lily turf produces scads of purple spikes. Seasonal highlights fill odd corners. A gordonia was placed in a corner bed to eventually hide the neighbouring roofline. Gardenias fill the shadier parts near the house while Chinese star jasmine fills gaps between the cypresses.

Repetition unifies and defines garden spaces, especially in a small garden. Along the exposed edge of the garden is a row of silver-leafed Leyland cypress known as 'Silver Dust', a fast-growing and tough competitor in a difficult situation. They form a dramatic line of architectural interest viewed from the living room. In time, they will be trained into columns to form a structural line that softens and defines the fence and perimeter.

Plants

'Silver Dust' is a selected form of x *Cupressocyparis leylandii*, the well-known and worrisome hybrid cypress that seems to be taking over the world. Originally known as 'Leighton's Green', it was a hybrid between *Chamaecyparis nootkatensis* and *Cupressus macrocarpa*, both of which are relatively well behaved.

Gordonia axillaris, originally from subtropical South Asia, is a small tree for small gardens. It has the unflattering common name of fried egg plant. Its autumn flowers drop face side up, often carpeting the ground around it.

Cherry pie (*Heliotropium arborescens*) is a low, spreading bush (height 1 metre, width 1.5 metres) with deep purple, pale mauve or white flowers.

Lamb's ears (*Stachys byzantina*) is an excellent weed suppressant but can be affected by high summer humidity. Clear out lower leaves as they die to prevent rotting around the stems and roots. Divide plants in autumn.

Plectranthus 'Mona Lavender' grows to about 50 centimetres and produces massed sprays of purple flowers in summer and autumn. The leaves have dark, wine-coloured undersides and glossy topsides making the plant attractive even out of bloom. It grows in shade and part shade, preferably in moist soil.

Roofs and Balconies

The conversion of this old Melbourne factory into apartments has provided several useful outdoor spaces for a garden to flourish, but sun is limited and conditions can be hard. This light well was designed with a minimalist aesthetic because the problems of watering and low light precluded good growth from most plants. The door is an antique Chinese artefact used to give a false perspective. Some would not classify this as a garden due to the absence of plants, but it qualifies as an outdoor space that lets light into the interior and provides a view out into the world. It creates an exciting mix of new and old.

Roof gardens are as old as history itself. Babylon had its Hanging Gardens around 600 BC; the Romans had them; and in Mexico, the Aztecs grew crops and ornamentals on their stepped pyramids.

Today, roof areas are an underused resource. Often left bare and desolate, they can be sunny oases, pumping life into polluted air and providing a pleasant respite from bitumen and built structures.

If the roof garden is not already part of the construction, you will need to adhere to engineering and construction standards and get strata and council approval. Older buildings may not have been built to support the added weight involved in a rooftop garden (soil, moisture etc.). Newer buildings are stronger and incorporate membranes that are effective in preventing leaks, the most common problem with roof gardens.

Rooftop Solutions

Gardening on a roof or a balcony can be difficult. Rooftops are windier, and sun on a roof is, literally, a burning issue. A roof garden exposed to the full force of the western sun will bake, and evaporation is greater than in a normal garden.

Shade Most roofs are above the tree level so there is rarely any natural shade. The solution is to make some. An umbrella might look good, but one strong gust and it's up, up and away. A permanent structure, such as a pergola covered with tough vines, is a lot safer. A pergola also provides a secure structure on which to attach a canopy, usually canvas or a synthetic shade material.

Soil Seek professional advice on the best soil to use. Ordinary garden soil is not suitable for a roof garden. It's heavy both wet and dry, and it compacts when it dries out. Landscaping companies supply light, open mixes rich in humus.

Planting If you are not able to build planters, use plain plastic pots linked by drip irrigation and disguised by sleepers and massed groundcovers, such as tough mondo grass. And to keep your plants healthy use organic fertilisers.

Space Leave room to move on a roof. Balance built objects with open space to keep it uncluttered. For entertaining, free up as much space as possible to encourage a relaxed ambience.

Roof Style

Much roof gardening is actually exterior decorating and there is more scope to let fantasy take over. A theme garden on the ground can often look out of place, but up here, the sky is the limit. A Balinese, Moroccan or desert oasis theme is easier to achieve when the surroundings do not dictate style.

Experiment with different moveable surfaces, for example pebbles or timber. Add to the ambience with a self-contained water feature. These come complete with fountains, bowls and other paraphernalia needed to bring the sight and sound of water to a roof or balcony. Use the walls for decorative treatments such as trompe l'œil—an illusory wall painting (see Illusions on page 204)—wall plaques and perspective panels that give an impression of depth.

Plants for Rooftops

Plants on a roof need to be tough. Choose plants that will bend in the wind rather than those with brittle stems; choose drought-hardy over tender plants. Check with your local nursery for suitable plants; before you shop, collect as much information as you can about the aspect, hours of sun, and wind force and direction on your roof.

Spring brings blue convolvulus and lavenders, while erigeron daisy, Chinese star jasmine and *Grevillea biternata* add white or cream touches.

This space on the other side of the apartment from the picture opposite has been given a Mediterranean touch. It is furnished with large terracotta tubs and a blend of edible plants, including espaliered lemons, and potted ornamentals, turning a barren space into a productive one. Large troughs containing herbs have been mounted on the wall to improve access to sun. A collection of architectural plants—soft yuccas (*Yucca elephantipes*), tough plants happy in low light, and a cardboard cycad (*Zamia furfuracea*)—give it visual appeal from the living room. A container-grown wisteria is being trained along the upper railing to provide some privacy from the prying eyes of neighbours.

Rooftop Casbah

Islamic style has always had a presence in our gardens. Mostly it stems from the form rather than the function of the traditional Islamic garden and that is certainly true in this case. But there is another factor working here that brings it closer to the origins of the style. Being a roof garden, it replicates the hot, dry desert spaces from whence the Islamic garden tradition arose. The challenge was to create a paradise, a place of respite and serenity.

In this garden, the long roof space is divided into more intimate sections by several design devices—patterning on the floor, and low borders and hedging delineate spaces. Stone pavers provide a neutral unifying backdrop.

Ornamental features all conform to a classical European or Middle Eastern theme. Turkish taps and Moroccan tiles on the water feature blend with iron urns and busts of another age.

Keeping Cool

A wrought-iron frame pergola is redolent of a Bedouin tent and houses canvas canopies that can be strung out to provide shade on hot days. Its rusted tan colour is echoed in the fabric used on the chair cushions. Iron was a popular material in the nineteenth century, and structures like the Eiffel Tower in Paris, the Crystal Palace in London, and the great railway stations of the Victorian age elevated it to an art form. It was also a time when the West was most closely engaged with what was then described as the Near East or Middle East, so in that sense its use is entirely appropriate.

Design Elements

Style For such a statement to succeed, it must be maintained throughout the garden, which is divided into entertaining and decorative spaces. The fountain uses antique Turkish taps as spouts and the backing tiles are modern copies of old Moroccan designs in a muted but bold colour pattern of tan, ochre, turquoise and off-white. Classical urns and pots work well in this fusion of Islamic and Western traditions.

Small Space Tips

Colour To maintain a unified theme, avoid strong colours but don't do away with colour altogether. The strong tan works as a highlight and complements the colours in the fountain and tiled wall plaques.
Espalier is a good technique for small spaces, especially walled gardens, as it spreads the green along the vertical planes, creating a classic style.

Unity Hedges and formal topiary plantings unify the design. The hedges run the entire length of the space and are given impetus by layering of different plant materials. For instance, a diamond-shaped carpet of dwarf mondo grass sits well with the geometry of the hedge lines, which zigzag around the fountain.

Plants

Box, lillypilly and escallonia were the main choices. The formal planting is comprised mostly of hedges and small trees that can be clipped to shape. Flower colour is mostly white.

Magnolia 'Little Gem' is a small-growing magnolia with large, fragrant white flowers over many months of the year.

Escallonia exoniensis 'Frades' is a tough dwarf plant for dry soil. Grow it as a hedge trimmed to shape. Escallonias have glossy leaves and prolific flowers in red, pink, cerise or white. This form grows 80 centimetres tall and wide, and has dark pink flowers all summer, even through winter in warm spots.

Japanese box (*Buxus microphylla* var. *japonica*) is a tough little plant for balconies. It is probably the most widely used hedging plant. Its smaller leafed relative, *Buxus microphylla* var. *microphylla*, is ideal for finer small-scale hedges.

Camellia sasanqua is one of the best choices for espalier treatment. Choose a single-stemmed nursery plant with evenly spaced branches that come off the trunk at near enough to right angles. This will make training much easier. Look for supple and willowy branches which are still strong enough to take the manipulation needed to shape the form.

Top left: Moroccan tiles form the backdrop to an attractive fountain.
Top right: A metal-framed pergola adds depth to the rooftop garden.
Bottom right: Raised beds are heavily planted with essentially green plants for year-long appeal. Seasonal bloomers add colour through flowers.

Tiled mosaics (below left) add sumptuousness to the overall design and bring a touch of interior design to the exteriors.

Atmospheric
Spaces

The sensory is the forgotten factor in many gardens— water flowing over a ledge, grass rustling in the wind, dry leaves crackling underfoot, chimes tinkling and velvety leaves brushing against you. These experiences are crucial to the ambience and atmosphere of a garden. When space is at a premium they add an important extra dimension.

The following pages look at some ways to make the most of these things and show how some people have sought to introduce a sense of restfullness into their gardens. Sometimes the path to repose and tranquility is conventional, with restful colours, gentle water features and safe garden patterns; other times it takes a dramatic left turn. What works for you? You may be surprised that convention is not always the way to sensory harmony.

Sanctuary and Senses

Above: Palms waving in the breeze.
Opposite: A swimming pool becomes a desert oasis.

The garden has become a place to chill out, revive and replenish mind, spirit and body—a sanctuary. Sanctuary can mean many things, but for the city gardener with little space it is a haven, a place to retreat from the world.

The move towards establishing gardens as sanctuaries is the same as that which has been motivating the sea-change phenomenon of recent years. In the same way that some people crave the smell of the ocean, fresh air and the feel of sand beneath their toes, familiar from summer holidays, others crave calming gardens of fragrant plants, cooling shade and resort-style amenities. The country hideaway—the 'tree change'—has the same connotation: the scent of eucalyptus, the warm humusy smell of a forest after rain and endless wide-open views of rolling fields or forest.

The act of gardening is restorative enough but a true sanctuary is also a sensory experience. When we think of the garden as sanctuary there is often a headlong rush of emotion or sense of recapturing some vestige of our past.

What Makes a Garden a Sanctuary?

Ambience, sensory appeal and a sense of place are three necessary ingredients to create your own backyard sanctuary.

Ambience is hard to define and can be as simple as a vague feeling of being somewhere special. What is important is getting the essentials right, whether it's a ferny nook, a shady tree or a stone pathway.

Sensory appeal What presses your buttons? Is it scented flowers or fragrant leaves? Is it the gentle lapping of a pool as a fountain splashes gently? Is it the quietude that comes with leaves rustling in the breeze? Is it the fresh, cloying smell after rain, the swishing of grasses or the cracking of bark, twigs and dried gum leaves? These feelings are ephemeral and personal so follow your heart.

Sense of place A garden attuned to its environment will always have a head start, whether it's a rainforest glade, a coastal heath or a dry bushland scene. Each can be a sanctuary as long as it sits peaceably with its surroundings.

To get the three, you will need to work with the elements and blend them seamlessly. Here are some ideas to work with:

Foliage A sanctuary is often an enclosed, hidden or private space. Use 'living umbrellas', plants that hide, protect and shield you. Picture a path lined with small trees suited to your climate—spreading crepe myrtles, a row of frangipani or angel's trumpets, Japanese maples, laburnum or *Camellia sasanqua*. Imagine

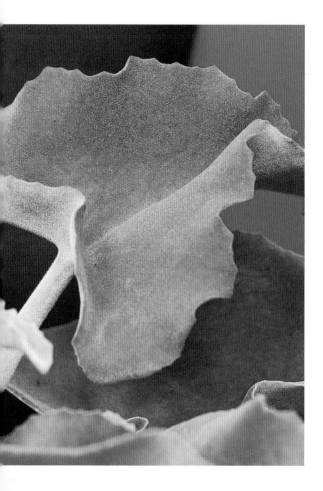

the branches just clearing your head, almost blocking out the sun but filtering light so it flickers and flares around you.

Space Into this partially enclosed grove of trees, an open sunny space comes to us from antiquity. Then, you might find a rudimentary altar or a stone seat encircled by benches. The more prosaic modern barbecue and chairs offer a similar scenario today.

Decorative elements include religious symbols we have borrowed from other cultures, such as Balinese flags and the colourful of umbrellas that have significance in Hindu ceremony. Incense, candles and flares (which can have a practical use by repelling insects!) are also part of many rituals.

Smell Incense is calming, but so are perfumed flowers. Grow frangipani and gardenia in frost-free regions. In temperate climes, grow sweet olive (*Osmanthus fragrans*) and daphne for their winter blooms. In summer, dry heat releases the essential oils in herbs and conifers.

Water is the life-giver revered in the ancient gardens of the Persians, Romans and Arabs. It still has a potent force. Use shallow pools, wall fountains and bowls of water to calm, add a reflective quality or introduce space into the garden. A pond is a void, accepted as a no-go area, and has an almost mystical quality, important for creating a sense of sanctuary.

Texture We love to touch plants. The tactile, wiry structure of waratah or

banksia flowers, the feathered tenderness of a protea, the velvety lamb's ear (*Stachys byzantina*), the silky undersides of *Costus barbatus* 'Red Tower' leaves and the peculiar coppery fuzz found under some rhododendron leaves and *Magnolia* 'Little Gem' all invite touch. Spiky plants like *Agave parryi*, *Aloe ferox*, various cactuses and euphorbias have different textural appeal, but don't invite touch. **Sounds** can be sublimely pleasing, for example water running or splashing over rocks, palm leaves and grasses rustling, Japanese temple bells and wind chimes. Some are almost imperceptible; others can be infuriating if not controlled.

How successful your sanctuary is depends on how well you blend the different elements. A subtle touch is often the best approach but do consider their interdependence. A bowl of water with floating candles, a grove of grasses beside a still pond, a set of temple gongs hanging from a frangipani branch—all work better in tandem.

Above: Flowering gardenias grown as a hedge provide a scented space for relaxing and reading.

OPPOSITE
Top: *Kalanchoe beharensis* has soft furry leaves that invite touch.

Bottom left: Water dripping into a bowl is cooling and refreshing.

Bottom right: A Buddha among tropical foliage is a calming touch.

A Study in Movement

Acontemporary, almost minimalist garden is the last place you would expect to find a series of sensual pleasures but this Melbourne garden combines the unexpected—formality with informality; billowing flowers and strong architectural shapes, water and stone. It is a blend of natural and built forms. Flowing water and inlaid pebbles give a sense of movement.

The garden forms an entrance courtyard to a large modern house. Entered along a colonnaded walkway, it is primarily a viewing garden. Paths are mainly for maintenance.

The small courtyard garden is beside the entrance to the house. It features clumps of kangaroo paws, kniphofia, giant white bird of paradise and a massed planting of carex grasses. All move in the breeze and the effect is enhanced by the gentle flow of water through the garden.

A gentle slope moves the water slowly so that glistening golden carex leaves catch the sun. They are a good match for the yellow poker cultivar 'James Nottle'. Pratia is planted between pavers to soften the edges.

Plants

The garden had to look good all year so the choice was a combination of bold structural plants softened by textured leaves and big-hearted, persistent bloomers.

Large white bird of paradise (*Strelitzia nicolai*) grow against the white-painted back wall, while drought-hardy, soft-tipped yucca (*Yucca elephantipes*) grow on the side wall. Overscaling is a useful tool in small gardens. One large sculpture or plant can look statelier than a group of smaller ones. Here the forms and the size of individual leaves convey the overscaling. The large leaves of strelitzia tend to eddy in the wind with a corkscrew motion, especially when the wind is strong.

To moderate these big architectural uprights, massed kangaroo paws (*Anigozanthos* 'Bush Dawn') flower most of the year, forming a dramatic colour fantasia. With them are large clumps of yellow pokers (*Kniphofia* 'James Nottle'), their golden blooms suffused with pale orange.

The vibrant yellow upright flowers of 'Bush Dawn' sway in the breeze and often bounce around when a small nectar-eating bird lands on them. The yellow poker flowers bend to catch the sun in the dying days of the summer. Brownish golden sedges (*Carex buchananii*) tone in with the yellow flowers, adding their own textural colour year-round.

Water

The water is the first element that attracts your attention. The pond starts in one corner and follows a dogleg path, emptying into a large rectangular pond that runs the length of the garden. Four pavers act as stepping stones providing a crossing that continues into the garden. The meandering shape of the watercourse is lined with river pebbles. The shallow water creates ripples as it trickles over the pebbles, slowing down as it travels and cascading over a stone causeway. The faint sound of flowing water accentuates the atmospheric nature of this garden.

Flooring

Sandblasted Gattistone pavers 'Murray' (50 x 50 centimetres) have a natural finish like stone. They are good around pools because grip is maintained in wet conditions. The pavers form stepping stones through the garden and border an inlay of pink broken sandstone applied in a crazy paving style. Broad sweeps of grey river pebbles add extra texture and interest.

At a Glance	
Complexity	Moderate
Ability	Design professional
Maintenance	Low

Sculpting a Garden

This dramatically different garden of upturned red sandstone landforms at unbelievable angles looks at first sight like a giant earthquake has hit the Red Centre. The plants—soft green and grey succulents and grasses—are drought tolerant and dry adapted, proving that a dry landscape can be as appealing and interesting as a lush, water-guzzling one.

The garden may look like an exploded Uluru, but the story surrounding its development has nothing to do with any violent geological uplifts. It was inspired by a mysterious piece of Northern Territory rock left in the designer's office, and the red sandstone was quarried near Alice Springs and cut and fitted on site. Rubble produced when the stone was cut was tumbled in a cement mixer until the sandstone formed smooth edges. The resulting gravel was used as groundcover in some parts of the garden, adding greater depth to the design.

The site is on a ridge with broad harbour views, so preserving its openness and utilising its light, especially the sunset, was important. The garden is viewed principally from inside the contemporary house, so framing of the upturned stone shelves was paramount. A large picture window opens onto a paved patio edged with poa grass and fine pea gravel.

An irregular-shaped pond, reminiscent of a pool in a Northern Territory canyon, is formed where several upturned rock slabs intersect. Water seems to flow beneath the earth from a subterranean reservoir.

The overall garden is a stunning blend of art and horticulture.

A Garden to be Seen

The modern house needed a sympathetic garden design that would look its best when viewed from the house. This design creates a dramatic scene that can be viewed like a stage set, where the recurring themes of the four elements—earth, fire, air and water—play out.

Shallow Soil

Shallow, sandy soil with a rock slab underneath prevented the use of large trees. The upturned rocks allow a measure of verticality that would otherwise be provided by plantings like trees and shrubs. The shallow-rooted succulents and grasses have sufficient soil depth to thrive.

Design Elements

Theme The design idea evolved from drawing after seeing the desert sandstone sitting in the office.

Structure Because the bottom rocks of a wall are critical for support, the corner rocks were cut first and the design developed from these. The elevated platforms were designed to provide adequate drainage.

Boundaries High sandstone walls elevate the garden above the street. The garden is revealed only after mounting wide steps from the street. Lillypilly hedges screen the garden on the street side.

Plants

The planting was largely determined by the rocky site and the owner's interest in succulents. The grey and green grasses and succulents were the perfect complement to the desert sandstone, with its kaleidoscopic colour changes in different light intensities. Among the plants are beds of *Festuca glauca*, borders of echeverias, cotyledons and agaves contrasting with ponytails (*Beaucarnea recurvata*).

The selection and positioning of plants is an important element. The focus is on shape, texture and form. Key species such as the agave (*Agave attenuata*), echeverias, and the deep red *Aeonium arboreum* 'Zwartkop' form distinctive rosettes, while the more upright euphorbias and ponytails (*Beaucarnea recurvata*) are positioned like sculptures to balance the stone pillars.

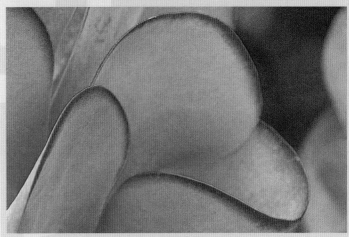

Top: The uplifted terraces are a good planting bed for succulents and grasses.

Above: *Kalanchoe* 'Flapjacks'.

At a Glance

Complexity High
Ability Design professional
Maintenance Low

A Reposeful Garden

This garden blends some of the great strands of garden design—European woodland, Japanese Zen and Islamic water motif— yet remains true to its location. The terrace backyard has been transformed with a magnificent wall of weathered sandstone, once part of the estate of a long-demolished John Verge early colonial mansion, 'Brougham'.

The architect's design for the interior freed up outside space, allowing the garden to assume a more traditional role, that of viewing and strolling. With the glass doors open, the room looks and feels like the outdoors, leaving the garden free of the clutter of outdoor dining settings.

The garden's design is essentially formal and symmetrical. Bluestone paving, a central pond and a copse of trees softened by a single groundcover establish the sense of sanctuary.

The pool is another restful element. Small and lying flush with the paving, its fountain is barely noticeable, adding ripples and a quiet gurgle, the perfect accompaniment to the rustle of leaves in a light breeze. A strip of sandstone ties it to the wall behind and makes a handy place to sit and dangle the feet after a hot, sultry summer's day. Omitting the sandstone capping from the two short ends makes the pool appear longer.

A conventional courtyard is open in the middle with perimeters filled in. By placing the pool in the centre—an unusual choice—the designer created real and perceived space around it.

Design Elements

Theme The blending of Asian elements with Western architecture and plantings—a kind of spiritual fusion between East and West—achieves simplicity and serenity. The signature sandstone wall so typical of Georgian Sydney is used to perfection. The design is pared back to emphasise this unique architecture and its formality is softened by Eastern restraint.

Services Bins have been built into cupboards at the front of the terrace where space was not used. Clothing is dried in dryers, rather than requiring an outdoor washing line.

Scale The planting is kept in proportion to the overall size of the garden. Placing the pond and garden beds in the centre makes space seem bigger and uncluttered. Big pots and the copse of trees all seem out of scale but this is intentional.

Flooring Large pavers in a small space make the space seem larger. Haddonstone bluestone pavers measure 45 x 45 centimetres.

Colour The colours play a major role in our perception of peace and also of space. A subdued palette of soft greens, olive or bronze shades makes the walls recede and enlarges the space. The pale green on the sidewalls accentuates the textures and colours of the sandstone.

Sculpture One single sculpture by Robert Klippel is the perfect companion to both sandstone and the plants. Large imported pots from Anduze, France were painted green to match the walls.

Plants

Silver birch (*Betula pendula*) is not generally considered a suitable tree for Sydney and several have been replaced. Nevertheless their white trunks work well here, at least while young and whippy. The potted sago palms (*Cycas revoluta*) from East Asia have a stand-alone architectural quality. *Liriope* 'Evergreen Giant' softens the pavers and hides the base of the paving and pool. It has smart purple flowers in autumn.

The centre of attention in a high-walled terrace garden is directed inwards with the rectangular pond and planting.

Right: An unusual focal point of the garden from inside, the convict-built stone wall adds a beautiful tonal quality to the simple, minimalist planting scheme.

At a Glance

Complexity Moderate

Ability Design professional

Maintenance Low

An Oasis of Calm

Located in a tightly packed pocket of inner-city Sydney, this totally enclosed courtyard is long and narrow but it feels much bigger than it is. It is quiet and calm and its green foliage gives it a subtropical lushness. This secret courtyard garden is hidden behind an older terrace house and has access to a rear lane. The cosy garden skirts a narrow section of the house, and includes a large outdoor dining space under a pergola adjacent to the house. The owner's own sculptures are displayed on the walls and the garden is rich with visual highlights beyond the verdant planting. This earthly paradise is filled with fragrant vines. There is a leopard tree and others which are scaled to the garden.

Design Elements

Theme The provision of a comfortable and comforting space is paramount in the evolution of this garden. It has a traditional planting scheme, with vines and climbers on the side walls and a mature leopard tree (*Caesalpinia ferrea*) offering shade from the western sun.

Space The space is uncluttered and open.

Flooring The choice of brick paving owes much to the Victorian heritage of the suburb and the house. The wave pattern disguises the elongated nature of the block. The eye tends to follow the waves as they pass from one wall to the other.

Boundaries The house itself forms one boundary but the high brick wall abutting the neighbour's property needed softening. This has been achieved by disguising it with vines such as *Mandevilla laxa*, which is deciduous in winter but green and perfumed in summer. This also gives a seasonal element as the garden changes considerably throughout the year.

Balance Vines arch over the pergola at one end, framing the view and creating a visual balance with the side planting at the opposite end.

The narrow garden is partially enclosed by a pergola supporting a grapevine.

Above: Unity comes from the neutral colour scheme, massed foliage and a few white flowers. The wavy brick pattern makes the space appear bigger.

Left: The undulating garden edge mirrors the patterning of the brick paving.

At a Glance

Complexity Low

Ability Enthusiastic amateur

Maintenance Moderate

Mood with Colour and Texture

This tiny garden of a single-storey period weatherboard house comprises a narrow front entrance and an oddly shaped rear section on two levels. Its appeal comes from its bold, unexpected colours.

Remember the old Rolling Stones lyric, 'I see a red door and I want it painted black'? Well, the owner of this stylish garden did just that, along with the walls of the house. The black is softened by aubergine garden walls at either end of the space and by the addition of simple container plantings and decorative elements. The black gives the area a formal edge, which is appropriate for a balanced entry space.

Old brick paving adds a patina of age and blends with surrounding houses in its historic precinct. The space is simply furnished, with a narrow bench and a garden bed filled with *Gardenia* 'Florida'. A thick screen of Chinese star jasmine (*Trachelospermum jasminoides*), a versatile climber that forms a hedge-like cover over the gate, ensures privacy. White shutters add a lighter touch to the black walls.

The aubergine colour scheme is repeated in the rear. This is a more informal space so there is no black. This section is on two levels: the bottom is devoted to car parking and the top level is little more than a balcony-sized space used for sitting and relaxing. A shade canopy covers part of the roof space, with five vertical stainless steel wires providing support for more star jasmine. Along the side, more wires support vines that provide privacy from the neighbours.

Above: A colourful ceramic warrior.

Left: A water bowl filled with pebbles and a glazed Chinese face adds a light touch in the front garden.

Opposite Top: A ceramic snail 'slithers' over a mossy ledge near a wall fountain.

At a Glance	
Complexity	Low
Ability	Design professional
Maintenance	Low

Design Elements

Colour Black, aubergine and other dark purples may seem dull on their own but they are lifted by the green foliage. Purples are strong, sophisticated colours that give a small space depth and complexity.

Ornamentation Pots, bowls of water, decorative pieces and the simple placement of a flower can provide complexity in a small garden without impinging on space.

*B*old, unexpected colours characterise this stylish garden. Old brick paving adds a patina of age and blends with surrounding houses in its historic precinct.

Functional
Spaces

Regardless of size, gardeners find a way to have their gardens fulfil many different functions. For some, a particular hobby or interest drives the design. For others, the garden is a work place or at least must fulfil some specific purposes. Small gardens especially need creative solutions to problems.

Moving from a large garden to a smaller townhouse or unit garden can be daunting, as we tend to take our existing practices with us. However, a small garden has its own characteristics and problems that must be overcome.

This chapter looks at some working gardens—gardens that fulfil a dream or serve a purpose for their owners.

A Cook's Garden

It's time to shake off the image of the old-fashioned kitchen garden. No longer relegated to an unseen backyard corner, this productive vegetable garden takes centre stage and is the main focus of the backyard. It fills the view from the newly renovated interiors and has a stylish outdoor eating area, which even incorporates an outdoor kitchen with sinks, a refrigerator and cooking facilities. The bright cerise paint job and antique Balinese door give it a classy edge.

The design stemmed from alterations made to the original old Californian bungalow. A new open-plan room at the rear helped to create a modern interior/exterior transition, with a new outlook onto the garden.

Inspired by the classical vegetable plot in the parterre style, the garden comprises two beds on the level area, edged with slate and connected by paths of white gravel. On the far side a raised bed is planted with taller vegetables so they do not shade the lower ground. Figs and lemons are espaliered along the fence of the narrow side passage and additional herbs grow in pots along the gravel path.

Although close to the coast, the garden is largely protected from the worst of the salt-laden winds. The warm coastal microclimate allows many warm-season edibles to be grown even in winter.

At the beginning of a new season the bean supports stand empty but access is always assured through a series of gravel paths. Raised beds support herbs and other vegetables.

Improving the View

The garden is in a heavily built-up area and the view of neigh-bouring blocks of flats was not very inspiring. Taller vegetables were planted in a raised bed on the eastern side, which is also the back of the garden. The raised bed helps hide many of the buildings and by planting on a north–south axis, the taller vegetables such as beans, okra and Jerusalem artichokes do not shade the other beds.

Outdoor Dining

The owner enjoyed entertaining friends and cooking and this role had to be incorporated in a stylish way. The southern edge of the property was selected for the dining pavilion. An ornate carved Balinese door forms the backdrop, with access to the side passage. The dining space is protected from the weather by a pergola made of polycarbonate roof sheeting, disguised by slatted timber under the roof. The pergola has an inbuilt pitch so the water will run off. If you want the battens to sit flush with the top of the beams they need to be rebated in. This will allow you to put your sheeting over the top without any bumps.

Garden Requirements

Materials Cowra gravel was used for the paths, and sawn slate capping for the pond and vegetable bed. The walls of the build-ing were made from recycled bricks thickly rendered with Mac Render to get an even surface. It is an acrylic finish suitable for coastal locations.

Sun and aspect The north-easterly aspect, an elevated position and few trees or overshadowing properties mean the rear yard is sunny and open, thus maintaining optimum conditions for food production—vegetables need sun to grow well and fast. Full sun is considered to be four to six hours per day, depending on the season.

Soil Vegetables grow best in a standard loam but clay and sandy soils can be improved with large quantities of organic matter such as humus, rotted animal manures or compost. This garden had been a building site where clay and rubble were brought to the surface. It was cleared away and replaced with fresh soil to a depth of 30 centimetres. A commercial vegetable and seeding mix with Nitro-Humus—a recycled sewage sludge high in organic matter—was used. These are available in bulk from landscape supply companies.

Top: At one end of the garden, a service area provides for food preparation and cooking and includes a covered dining space.

Above: A harvest from the garden.

At a Glance

Complexity Medium

Ability Skilled amateur

Maintenance High

The area at the top of the sloping garden is used as an exhibition space for large works. The structure at the side is the old garage, used as an outdoor studio.

A Gallery Garden

There are those who not only live in but also work in their gardens. This sculptor's studio is a converted garage and the garden doubles as a gallery.

Stairs wend their way down from the top of this small, steep garden. The transitions are quite abrupt, the first turning at a right angle onto a cantilevered timber boardwalk. They form a descending series of private, quiet spaces, providing plenty of scope for displaying artworks of varying dimensions.

A water wall is the garden centrepiece but it is not a loud, attention-seeking water feature. All that is heard is a quiet sound of running water.

Right: Display areas along the descent down can be seen at the top and bottom of the stairs. This gravelled space is for larger pieces.

A Space for Scupture

There were no useable outdoor spaces. The size of the sculptor's work was increasing. She needed space to store pieces between exhibitions but the site was difficult, small and very steep. The space had to work as a gallery.

A landscape architect created a series of terraces, platforms and steps tacking down the slope. Visitors pause and enjoy the sculptures, each in its own discrete space. Surfaces define each exhibition space, and the path progresses through a series of narrow ledges, steps and wider projections that abut the pathway and steps. At certain points, shelves projecting onto the pathway signify turning points to provide new focal points.

Access for Cranes

Cranes needed to be able to access the garden to lift and remove large, heavy artworks.

The entrance to the garden is at street level and the wall to the garden was set back from the alignment. Extra-large pieces are displayed on the footpath but within the property boundary. Delivery of materials and the removal of finished sculptures are achieved by a crane.

Small Space Tips

Illusion A zigzagging pathway down a steep slope creates the perception of more space.

Different platforms allow works to be displayed on all levels.

Design Elements

Space organisation is crucial in this garden. It is a series of integrated spaces which double as platforms, display spaces and walkways.

Lighting adds versatility to the design. The lights throughout the garden can be manipulated to highlight different types and sizes of sculpture.

Materials and texture Large concrete walls define the space and screen the different levels. Concrete, wood and steel give a contemporary, hard-edged feel, while varying gravels—including a coarse sandstone mulch at the bottom of the descent, round river pebbles at the top and fine gravel near the house—help define spaces. To create the surface of the water wall, blue metal chips were affixed to an epoxy resin on concrete sheeting. Small pieces of glass embedded in the concrete catch the light and sparkle.

Sound The water wall is angled away from the vertical. If it had not been so, water would have splashed into the reflecting pool at the base. Instead, water runs gently down over the raised surface of the wall and is then recycled.

Line and transition A steel gate opens to reveal a choreographed pathway leading through, down and across the sloping front yard. The drop is broken into many slight changes of level.

Mystery and surprise The paths change direction and move from one side of the garden and one level to another. This provides new viewpoints which double as display areas for sculpture.

Colour Colours used here are muted and reflect the natural tones of sandstone and angophora bark. Muted pink, ochre and green on the walls reflect colours on the house and the trees. Lighting accentuates this at night.

Plants Plants are secondary in this design and were chosen to not overwhelm the site. They are mostly native plants including Sydney red gum (*Angophora costata*), Gymea lilies, tree ferns and other small native ferns.

A wall fountain is a permanent ornamental feature.

At a Glance	
Complexity	Difficult
Ability	Professional landscape architect
Maintenance	Low

A Home Office Garden

It is becoming increasingly common to have a separate home office or even a granny flat in the backyard. An attractive garden can enhance working conditions and present a pleasing reception space for clients and colleagues. But building a separate structure in the garden usually results in a reduced garden area that demands a dual perspective and often a complete revamp.

This photographer's home garden functioned as a studio for photographing plants and as a meeting place. It was particularly important for someone working in an aesthetic medium to create surroundings conducive to productivity.

Tucked into the rear garden of a small Federation semi, this home office was given a pleasant garden outlook and space for reading over a cup of tea. It provides a relaxed atmosphere to meet with clients.

A Multi-purpose Garden

The garden needed to look good and work as a place to relax and entertain on weekends and evenings, as well as supporting the photographer's work. The garden in front of the office could have become simply a walkway if not handled sensitively.

This office was built at the rear of a semi-detached house in the inner city. It has wide glass windows facing onto the space and the only solution was to create a small courtyard that offered an attractive approach but also a multifunctional retreat.

Plants in Containers

A large box elder (*Acer negundo*) shaded the area so it was cool in summer yet sun filtered through in winter. Neither grass nor garden beds were an option and the aspect demanded largely shade-loving plants.

The owner was a real plantaholic so the solution was to grow many favourite things in pots. A collection of succulents is displayed on shelves against the house in the sunniest position. Plants that thrive in shade or partial sun were selected, and those that needed more sun were moved in summer to improve chances of survival. Low brick walls provide a place for containers to be displayed and protect many of the existing shrubs such as a large *Murraya paniculata* and apricot *Brugmansia suavolens*.

Even though pots are a mix of glazed and unglazed containers, they are tied together by burgundy and green glazes that mimic the exterior paint colours. The terracotta pots also blend with the paving bricks.

Seasonal flowers, foliage colour and varied leaf shapes provide the main plant interest here.

Above right: Planting in pots and installing display shelves on the wall of the house overcame limited space.

Design Tips

Group plants according to needs Hardy sun-loving succulents prefer the sunniest positions. Leave shadier spots for foliage plants that need less sun. Group plants that need constant moisture and more humid conditions separately from those that prefer a drier atmosphere; the combined effects of watering and plant transpiration will create a warm, humid microclimate. The temperature stays higher in winter, enabling a bigger range of plants to grow in this frost-free position.

Use colour to enhance design Place bright, warm colours like red, orange and yellow in the foreground; in the rear they make the space seem smaller. Kalanchoe, kangaroo paws and cannas are the most colourful; their reds and oranges stand out against the quieter blues and mauves.

Arrange pots to maximise light exposure Place the tallest plants at the back, or on the highest rungs of stepped stands. The higher pots act as a screen for privacy and keep the foreground open for smaller plants.

Design Elements

Flooring Brick paving suits the Federation style of the house, and its curved pattern follows the line of the retaining walls. This provides a neutral backdrop and allows the plants to shine.

Colour To tie in the new structure with the old, all the paling fences and the house and office were painted turquoise, a colour favoured by the impressionist artist Monet and copied by many others since. Turquoise sets off the greens of the foliage and gives it a lift especially where trees cast a lot of shade. Turquoise is also a rare flower colour, only appearing in two plants that I can think of: southern star (*Tweedia caerulea*) and the jade vine (*Strongylodon macrobotrys*), a tropical beauty that only grows successfully in the far north. It is thus unlikely to clash with any floral colour scheme. This versatile colour exudes vibrancy; without it the space could have appeared dull and gloomy.

Opposite: Painting walls and fence in the single colour help to unify the space. Maintaining a distinctive colour scheme of flowers in mauves, pinks and deep reds further unifies disparate elements.

Blueberry ash is a small tree but it can be used as a hedge or clipped into shape. This pink-flowered form, *Elaeocarpus reticulatus* 'Prima Donna', is probably the best to use.

A collection of unusual rocks from inland Australia makes an interesting focal point.

Plants

Mixing foliage plants with weeping habits, erect foliage and coloured leaves gives the courtyard planting interest and contrast. In the sunniest corner, tall pots hold dragon's blood tree (*Dracaena draco*). Ponytail (*Beaucarnea recurvata*) is in the rear, and in the middle are coloured forms of New Zealand flax (*Phormium* cultivars) and soft yucca (*Yucca elephantipes*).

Native plants like *Acacia cognata* 'Green Mist' and *A. howittii* 'Green Wave', used as container plants, have a weeping or prostrate habit and dwarf form suitable for containers or bonsai culture. Also try *A. pravissima* 'Dwarf' and *A. cognata* 'Limelight'. Flowering is subordinate to foliage in most cases. Succulents and strap-leafed plants have fine, broad, thick, weeping and coloured leaf forms. Mix and match them so they give the arrangement movement and variety. Among the plants used are *Yucca elephantipes*, *Dracaena draco*, *Phormium* 'Maori Magic' series, *Agave attenuata*, *Strelitzia reginae* and *Beaucarnea recurvata*.

Pools For Small Gardens

Landscaping the pool area calls for sensible planting and plenty of forethought. Privacy, safety, beauty and convenience should always be the prime considerations. When choosing plants, examine such things as spread, leaf drop, flower fall and seed production. The increased enjoyment and added dollar value more than outweigh the time and effort you put into it.

This pool takes up most of the backyard but the addition of raised beds along the fence and a timber bridge makes access easier.

Plants

Plants soften the harsh lines of swimming pool equipment and help swimming pools to blend more naturally with the surrounding environment. Tall plants will form privacy screens around the pool area.

Choose low-maintenance plants. For instance, you don't want large deciduous trees around a swimming pool, as you'll end up fishing all those leaves out of the water! Even needle-bearing evergreen trees can be messy. Avoid fruit trees: not only are they messy, but the fruits attract bees. And as beautiful as flowers are, they too can be bee-magnets. Even worse, plants with invasive root systems—such as Chinese tallowwood (*Sapium sebiferum*), liquidamber, melaleuca, wisteria, holly and *Nerium oleander*—can damage a swimming pool over the years. Always avoid cocos palms (*Arecastrum romanzoffianum*), traveller's palm (*Ravenala madagascariensis*) and all phoenix palm species as these can crack the pool wall.

Use plants with large leaves not small ones, and big flowers that hang on or drop discretely. Avoid flowers like wattles, bottlebrushes and coarse, small petals that drop readily (peaches and cherries for instance), as petals and fine leaves can clog filters and collect on the bottom of the pool. Tannins in tea trees can also stain. Dipladenias, cordylines and acalyphas are good in warmer zones. Mexican mock orange (*Choisya ternata*) is good for southern regions.

If space for garden beds is limited around your pool, use pots of annuals or perennials to provide summer colour. Vines will grow happily on pool fencing.

Fencing

Fencing is a legal requirement around swimming pools in most States of Australia and is essential for the safety of small children. Some States insist on safety and first-aid instructions being prominently displayed. Check with your local council before starting any work. Plan carefully to incorporate regulations into your design as corrections can be costly.

The right fence design can also provide privacy. If you don't like the look of a fence, soften it by training vines to grow over it; the vines will also enhance privacy.

Toughened glass is the premium product (with a premium price) for pool fencing. New seamless forms allow

A spa or plunge pool is small enough to fit in many a small garden and can become an attractive feature. Here the owners have added a tiled backdrop in a loosely Mondrian-style rectilinear pattern.

full view of the surroundings. However, it needs regular cleaning. The smooth surface of the glass makes it hard for children to climb on (and therefore safer).

Fences should not have crossbeams that allow a child to climb over, nor should the spaces be wide enough for a foot to wedge in. Timber or steel fences with tall railings are a good choice and allow for creative designs.

Patios and Lighting

Patios provide not only beauty, but safety for swimming pool areas. A scarred concrete patio provides a slip-resistant surface to step onto when climbing out of the pool. If you opt for a brick patio instead, be sure to keep the surface of the bricks rough (you'll have to clean moss off patios periodically). For convenience around swimming pools, nothing beats a closed gazebo in which you can change into/out of your clothes and where you can relax in the shade. A patio can also accommodate barbecue equipment and outdoor furniture.

Timber decking provides an attractive addition to most pools and moss and algae are less likely to grow on it. Moss can establish in winter when there is less sun, but is easily scrubbed off with a stiff broom come spring.

Lighting around a pool is as much for safety as it is for amenity. A well-lit area reduces the risk of tripping over or falling into the pool in the dark.

Planted
Spaces

Small gardens demand more careful plant selection and a fair degree of discipline on the part of the garden owner.

Make it your goal to fashion a garden that looks good for most of the year but at the same time provides seasonal or monthly highlights. Downtime—that seasonal disorder that affects many gardens—can be avoided if you focus on the scale, size, spread and maintenance levels to ensure a relatively trouble-free garden. Every plant should earn its keep in a small space and plants that offer a show in more than one season are desirable. In cooler areas, evergreens and coloured foliage plants can add winter interest.

The following pages give general guidelines for selecting plants for the small garden, taking into consideration climate, aspect, soil, microclimates and maintenance. I have given broad principles for planting rather than comprehensive plant lists. There are examples of plants in different styles of garden and from this you may be able to extrapolate what sort of planting will suit your climate and conditions.

Choosing Your Plants

SMALL EXOTIC TREES for a woodland style are varied. Many flower in autumn, when there are often few flowers. **Clockwise from top left:** • *Magnolia grandiflora* 'Little Gem' is a dwarf form of the giant bull bay magnolia from southern United States. It prefers good moisture and is said to grow to 4–5 metres, though being a recent introduction, how it performs at 30–40 years is hard to say. • Gordonia or fried egg plant (*Gordonia axillaris*) from southern China is an attractive plant that can be grown as a large shrub or small tree. It prefers cool winters and warm summers. A newer introduction, *G. yunnanensis* prefers a cooler climate. • *Camellia sasanqua*. Sasanquas are drought hardy and versatile. They can be grown as trees, shrubs, screens or hedges as well as bonsai and topiary. • *Michelia yunnanensis*, a shrub or small tree, grows to 4 metres. It can be trained as a hedge or topiary. The flowers have a pleasant cinnamon scent. Grow it in part sun in an easterly position. It takes light frost only.

Climate, your lifestyle, garden style and local conditions determine what plants to grow.

Climate

Most plant failures are a result of trying to grow plants outside their natural conditions. Choose plants suited to your climate and you are more likely to be successful. In Sydney and Brisbane, for instance, it will be difficult to grow cool-climate plants from Melbourne or the Southern Highlands of New South Wales. In Melbourne and other southern regions, subtropicals or other plants that need warmer conditions in winter won't do well.

Neglected gardens offer clues as to what are the toughest plants to grow. If time is short, select these as backbone plantings. Even if doing your own landscaping and designing, it pays to call in a consultant horticulturalist who can provide you with information about places of origin and climatic growing zones.

Some nurseries list plants by water and climate requirements. You can also check latitude and continental positions of where plants grow. Check a good reference book or look up plants on the internet. You may need to include the word 'origins' to get the details you need. Another useful tip is to use 'growing conditions' with the name of the plant. Seek out plants that come from a latitude and location similar to your own as this gives a reasonable approximation to your local climate and plants are more likely to succeed.

Lifestyle

Choose plants that match your lifestyle. Many time-poor professional home-owners opt for 'low-maintenance' architectural and foliage plants that do not demand more than casual attention or occasional mulching.

If you love garden tinkering and have time to spare, go ahead and plant complicated schemes or fussier plants. Perennials, bulbs and annuals can take time but will reward you with brilliant displays of flowers that you don't get with foliage plants.

Planting Style

Planting style should reflect your lifestyle. If it does not say something about you then chances are you will not feel comfortable in it.

EDIBLE TREES

Clockwise from top left: • Lychee is suitable for warm frost-free climates, but it may need some protection from birds and bats who find the fruit as delectable as we humans. • Coffee is a surprising choice to many but the bush is a delight, with its bright red cherries, fragrant white flowers and glossy dark green leaves. It does best in areas with cool but not cold nights and warm days. • Apples need a cool climate with cold winters but there are some low-chill varieties like 'Pink Lady' and 'Granny Smith' that crop in warmer climates. • Pomegranate loves a Mediterranean climate with hot summers and cool, wet winters. Choose one of the newer Russian or Spanish cultivars for better flavoured fruit.

Plants and garden style go hand in hand. Do you prefer a formal or informal look? Do you want native plants alone or in conjunction with exotics? Are you prepared for the maintenance of a cottage garden or the downtime of a perennial garden? Do you want restful and calm or colourful and busy?

Soil Type

Have a look at your soil before you buy plants. If it is sandy, select plants adapted to poor sandy soils. If clay, look for plants that will thrive in it whether wet or dry. Clay can become hard and concrete-like in drought and slimy mud in the wet. Plants need to be able to survive these twin extremes. Adding organic matter will help both clay and sandy soil.

Use a soil-testing kit to determine the pH (acidity or alkalinity) of your soil. Plants grown in the wrong soil type may not be able to access soil nutrients. Alter soil pH by adding lime to acidic soil and sulphur to alkaline soil.

Acid-loving plants include azaleas, camellias, daphne, gordonia, gardenias, pieris and rhododendrons. Lilacs, ceanothus, philadelphus and bearded irises prefer alkaline soil.

Aspect, Sun and Shade

Ignoring aspect can lead to a garden that does not work. Mistakes include putting a sitting area in the spot that is coldest and shadiest in winter, or trying to grow shade-loving plants in the sun. Shade and sun vary with the season. Observe where

Deciduous Trees for Winter Sun and Summer Shade

Butterfly or orchid tree (*Bauhinia × blakeana*) WT, ST, T

Callery pear (*Pyrus calleryana*) including cultivar 'Bradford' CT, T

Cherries (*Prunus serrulata*)—the white cultivars are the best: 'Shimidsu Sakura' and 'Shirotae') CT

Crabapples (*Malus × floribunda*, *M. ionensis* 'Plena', *M.* 'Gorgeous' and *M.* 'Profusion') CT, WT

Crepe myrtles (*Lagerstroemia indica* and 'Indian Summer' series)

Dogwood CT, T

Forest pansy (*Cercis canadensis*) CT

Frangipani (*Plumeria rubra*) WT, ST, T

Fringe tree (*Chionanthus retusus* or *C. virginicus*) CT, WT

Golden robinia (*Robinia pseudoacacia* 'Frisia') CT, WT

Japanese maple (*Acer palmatum* and cultivars) CT

Judas tree (*Cercis siliquastrum*) T, CT, WT

Magnolia (*Magnolia denudatum*) CT, WT

Pistachio (*Pistacia chinensis*) CT, WT

Russian Olive (*Elaeagnus angustifolia*) CT

Silver Pear (*Pyrus salicifolia* 'Pendula') CT

Smoke Bush (*Cotinus coggygria*) CT

Weeping Silver Pear (*Pyrus salicifolia* 'Pendula') CT

WT = warm temperate
CT = cool temperate
T = tropical
ST = subtropical

GROUNDCOVERS

Left: *Scaevola aemula* 'Purple Fanfare' is a free-flowering groundcover particularly useful in coastal districts and in containers in small sunny courtyards.

Right: *Hardenbergia* 'Happy Wanderer' grows over most parts of Australia and is a light climber or groundcover. Some newer cultivars are more shrub-like. It flowers in spring.

the sun is in each season and where you need to introduce or minimise shade in summer or winter. This will have a major bearing on the viability of the plants you select. Sun lovers grown in shade will become weak and thin; sun will burn the leaves of shade lovers.

The orientation of the garden will have a major impact on what you can grow. In winter, the sun rises later and sets earlier and is lower in the sky than in summer. This means shadows are longer even in the middle of the day and the sun is less intense. Day length in the tropics hardly changes; further south it is marked. Tasmanians notice the change from the longer twilight hours of summer to the short days of winter possibly more than any other Australians.

The following outlines the characteristics of gardens with different aspects:

A north-facing garden is always the warmest location, enabling plants that suit warmer climates to thrive.

A south-facing garden will receive less sun, be cooler in summer and may be totally shaded in winter. Choose shade-loving woodland or alpine plants.

West-facing gardens receive afternoon sun and may be drier. Drought-tolerant Mediterranean plants for full sun may be suitable, but avoid 'woolly'-leafed plants as they can rot if cold dew lies on their leaves in winter.

East-facing gardens warm up quickly in the morning when the sun hits them but are cool on winter afternoons.

The number of hours of cold or heat during a day limits what we can safely grow in gardens. Look at weather charts of different locations in Australia and compare the average daytime temperatures of, say, Sydney, Melbourne and Brisbane. You may see little difference in maxima and minima but what these figures don't tell you is the time taken for the maximum temperature to be reached. Nor do they show how long each day the temperature hovers around that maximum figure.

In each case, it may be two to three hours before the temperature starts to climb from its overnight minimum. Gardens in more northerly regions therefore have a warmer ambient temperature than in cities further south. Where gardens in Brisbane may have an overnight minimum of 2°C, it only lasts for about half an hour, compared with several hours in Melbourne. This has a major impact on soil temperature and on what plants will successfully grow where. In spite of minimal difference in recorded temperatures, winter soil temperature is lower in Melbourne than Sydney and Sydney has cooler soil temperatures than Brisbane.

SMALL TROPICAL TREES AND SHRUBS

Clockwise from top left: • Sealing wax palm (*Cryostachys renda*) grows in tropical regions. • Frangipani (*Plumeria* x *rubra*) needs a warm, frost-free climate and full sun to flower well. • Golden shower tree (*Cassia fistula*) needs a warm climate but grows as far south as Sydney or Perth in frost-free locations. It is a large tree in the tropics but small out of normal range. • Crepe myrtle (*Lagerstroemia indica*) is a versatile small tree now also available as hybrids with a Louisiana species that is less prone to powdery mildew in humid regions. • Angel's trumpet (*Brugmansia versicolor*) is a beautifully fragrant plant that can be grown as a small tree. It flowers in the warmer months and may die back in colder climates, but generally regrows from the roots. • *Heliconia stricta* 'Tagami' grows in a clump to about 2.4 metres. All heliconias should be dug up and replanted every two or three years and the soil replenished as they quickly starve soils.

NATIVE TREES AND LARGE SHRUBS

Top row, from left: • *Banksia* 'Giant Candles' is a bushy hybrid form of *B. ericifolia* and *B. spinulosa*. It needs well-drained soil and full sun. •Queensland firewheel tree (*Stenocarpus sinuata*) is a tall but narrow tree suitable for small gardens but make sure there is room for the trunk to expand. • *Callistemon* 'Harkness' is one of the best miniature trees for a small garden. It takes pruning and flowers prolifically in spring and autumn. • *Corymbia* 'Summer Beauty' is a grafted hybrid of the flowering gum of Western Australia.

Middle row, from left: • The illyarrie or red capped gum (*Eucalyptus erythrocorys*) is a large tree in its native Western Australia but much smaller in the eastern States. • Bark of *Angophora costata*, a tree not normally recommended for planting in small gardens but commonly retained around newer ones.

Bottom row, from left: • Blueberry ash (*Elaeocarpus reticulatus* 'Prima Donna') is a pretty and versatile tree that stands some clipping. • Coast myall wattle (*Acacia binervia*) can be a shrub or small tree. It grows in shallow soils on heaths and in dry forests where its size is contained.• *Grevillea* 'Firesprite' is a long-flowering hybrid between *G. longistyla* and *G. venusta*. It is fast growing to 3–5 metres with a spread of 2 metres and is ideal for screening. • A young cabbage tree palm (*Livistona australis*) is good in a large container but generally too large and messy for smaller gardens.

SHRUBS

Top row, from left: • Abutilon or Chinese lantern is a pretty, free-flowering shrub in a broad range of colours, mostly in the warm spectrum of yellow to red. • *Leucospermum cordifolium* grows to about 2 metres high and 1.5 metres wide. It grows best in cool, dry climates and coastal sites but is not always reliable in hot humid climates like that of Sydney. • Tree begonia is an ideal soft-stemmed perennial plant for warm gardens. It grows like bamboo with the advantage of brilliant flowers and coloured bracts that last for months.

Centre row, from left: Bird of paradise (*Strelitzia reginae*) is a clump-forming perennial with flowers appearing from autumn to spring. • Vireya rhododendron is the so-called tropical rhododendron but it grows even in cold climates, as its natural habitat is high mountains. It is rarely good in humid coastal zones.

Bottom row, from left: • *Justicia carnea* is a subtropical perennial that can be trained as a hedge. It resents frost and prefers a moist but well-drained soil enriched with organic matter. • *Justicia brandegeana* or prawn plant is an old-fashioned plant set for renewal. Both it and the blue plumbago are here grown in a raised bed, a good idea as both spread by stolons or suckers.

Bottom right: • *Leucospermum saxosum* 'Mardi Gras® Ribbons' flowers in spring on a bush 2 metres high × 1.5 metres wide. It suits coastal conditions and containers.

Dark Shadows

Shadows cast by fences, walls and tall buildings are a constant issue for many small gardens. How seriously this will impact on your ability to establish a garden depends on the aspect and the position of the obstruction.

Dealing with the dark in small space gardens often requires use of lighter coloured foliage and flowers. Lime green or variegated leaves and white or light flowers too can help to bring light to dark corners. One option is to look upon the shady garden as a night-time space where night-flowering plants with white, often fragrant flowers show up in the moonlight. After all, this was the original purpose of Vita Sackville-West's white garden so empathically copied in the 1990s. She selected white flowers for a terrace garden specifically because it was primarily used at night for strolling and viewing. Only white flowers showed up in the gloom and the same is good for a space that is dark by day.

One lime green foliage plant is *Begonia* 'Baby Doll'. Light-coloured flowers to lighten dark corners include white-flowered honesty (*Lunaria annua* 'Variegata') and *Pittosporum* 'James Stirling'.

Water

Water is a hot issue so it pays to choose plants that can thrive on natural rainfall. Long-term drought in many parts of Australia means that many traditional thirsty garden plants are becoming less common and more expensive to maintain. Choosing drought-tolerant plants is the best option. Check

NATIVE PERENNIALS AND SHRUBS
Top row, from left: • Clumps of kangaroo paws (*Anigosanthos* x *flavidus*) are ideal in a raised bed. This cultivar is 'Yellow Gem'.
• Flannel flowers deserve to be grown far more than they are. They grow perfectly well in raised beds of sandy, humus-enriched soil without the addition of chemical fertilisers.
Bottom row: • *Grevillea thyrsoides* red stamens and blue–grey leaves.

with your local water authority to determine what watering systems are permissible.

Rain Patterns

Rainfall patterns are markedly different between Australia's east and west. Perth and Sydney have similar winter temperatures, as do Adelaide and Melbourne. However, Adelaide and Perth have Mediterranean climate patterns giving them a wet winter/dry summer pattern suited to Mediterranean and temperate-region plants from Australia and other locations with similar conditions. Melbourne has rain distributed more evenly through the year, with spring the wettest season, and is suited to plants described as preferring a warm or cool temperate climate. Sydney and Brisbane have moist summers and drier winters (though again with rain distributed throughout the year) more conducive to subtropical plantings. This is accentuated the further north you garden on the east coast.

SUBTROPICAL FOLIAGE SHRUBS

Top row, from left: • *Cordyline terminalis* hybrids come in many shades and most are more richly coloured in the winter months. • Red-edge dracaena (*Dracaena marginata*). • *Dracaena marginata* 'Tricolor' is most effective planted in large groups in the warmer garden. In cool areas, it makes a good container plant.

Bottom row, from left: • *Colocasia* 'Black Magic' grows in moist soil or in ponds. Its brilliant matt black foliage is a good foil for other plants, particularly lime green and variegated plants. It usually dies back in winter. • *Cordyline fruticosa* 'Wili's Gold'. • *Melianthus major* grows over a wide range of climates and has attractive foliage. It can be a weed in Western Australia.

Microclimates: Extending Your Range

A microclimate is a variation in the climate within a given area. Hills, hollows, built structures or nearby lakes or streams can create microclimates. For example, although walls can create problems for small garden owners due to the shade they cast, they also protect small spaces from the elements. Proximity to the coast raises the ambient temperature, enabling more tender plants to be grown.

Understanding microclimates will help you to grow plants way out of their normal range. A warm microclimate may allow you to grow tender plants in a frosty garden or tropical plants in a temperate one. Conversely, a cool microclimate may mean the difference between just admiring those winter tulips in someone else's garden and growing them yourself.

Many different microclimates may occur at the same time in different areas of a garden. The effect is probably more pronounced in urban situations—where paving and buildings act as heat sinks in the day, increasing the ambient temperature overnight—than in rural ones. A range of hills can create a rain shadow in one suburb, while one a few kilometres away can be positively equatorial. The most dramatic instance is when it rains across the street but your garden remains high and dry. Even the environment immediately surrounding a plant or bed can have very localised climate conditions compared to the rest of the garden.

Microclimates can lead to major variations in both the blooming time and quantity of flowers. Even within a garden, planting in protected corners, in raised beds or in improved soil can lead to vastly different results compared with the same plants growing in natural soil or in exposed positions.

Some preconditions will always point to the existence of microclimates within a garden:
- the southern side of a house is usually more shaded and less exposed to hot, dry winds
- the northern and western aspect of a house is hotter and more exposed to strong sunshine and hot westerly winds
- plants themselves create microclimates. For example, trees protect soil and unless the species are water guzzlers, the ground beneath should remain moist longer than in exposed positions.

Microclimate and Physical Features

Slopes and dips South-facing slopes protect plants below, while north- or west-facing slopes are prone to hot, dry conditions.

Water, including pools, moderates temperatures both in winter and summer.

Reflected heat from buildings, streets and driveways creates hot, dry conditions. Walls reflect heat, especially in summer; creepers help to reduce the glare.

Existing trees, depending on their spread and foliage type, can protect from frost, cool down hot spots and warm up cool spots.

Microclimate and Aspect

Northerly aspect

- Receives the most sunlight throughout the day as sun travels from east to west.
- Earliest growth and flowers after winter, i.e. spring comes earlier.
- Hot, dry conditions near walls, especially in summer.
- Not good for shade-loving plants unless cover is provided.
- Good for growing heat-loving plants in a cooler climate.

Easterly aspect

- The morning sun comes from the east so the ground warms more quickly in winter.
- Good for roses or broad-leafed plants.
- Generally a little cooler than north- or west-facing aspects.
- Plants may receive part or full shade in the afternoon.

Westerly aspect

- Full west-facing gardens receive the hotter afternoon sun and hence reflected heat.
- Often shaded in the mornings.
- Drying winds may be a problem.
- Perfect for plants that thrive on intense sunlight and dryness; all other plants need extra water, mulch or sun protection.

Southerly aspect

- Little direct sunlight in winter with more in summer.
- Growing season starts later after winter and finishes earlier in autumn.
- More even temperature than northern or western aspects.
- Good for cool- and shade-tolerant plants.
- Good aspect for growing cool, montane plants in a hotter climate.

Above: This garden in Sydney supports a range of temperate region and subtropical plants. The local microclimate is important but once the right plants are established, they help to create an even warmer microclimate. (See also pages 180–183.)

Opposite: A warm microclimate will support plants like snake plant (*Amorphophallus bulbifer*), *Globba winitii* and *Iresine herbstii*.

An Urban Paradise

The lush, coolness of the subtropical garden beckons, cajoles and entices us into its enveloping forest with a warm, inviting hug like that of a long-lost friend.

The two main features of this garden, a winding path of decomposed granite and a long wall fountain, are completely framed or partly obscured by the planting. The plantings present vivid contrasts and unexpected pairings. Alongside an Abyssinian banana, with its broad green upright leaves and the complementary giant lime green colocasia or elephant's ear (*Xanthosoma sagittifolium aureum*), dainty China roses such as *Rosa* 'Mutabilis', 'General Gallieni' or 'Old Bluish' mingle with perennials and groundcovers that originate in latitudes and continental aspects similar to Australia's east coast. In summer the garden thrives, with only a few weeks' downtime in late winter.

Too Much Moisture

The steeply sloping garden was frost free, with a constant flow of underground moisture and this played havoc with conventional temperate plantings. The conditions were more suitable for subtropical plants: subsurface moisture helps them thrive by increasing humidity and retaining permanent moisture. The cool subtropical microclimate has mild winters and warm, wet summers. Winters can be cool inland, but on the coast frost is unheard of. Summers are warm, humid and wet. Plants were selected that would do well in this hybrid temperate/subtropical climate.

Finding Plants to Suit the Climate

Plants that suit this climate are not among the more commonly sold plants in nurseries. The biggest challenge was finding which plants would make the best fit.

The designer eschews standard nursery lines for more unusual finds. This meant searching, often in non-standard nurseries and plant-friendly outlets such as local markets, specialist nurseries and from passionate collectors. It is this search that makes the garden such a labour of love. Begonias, bromeliads, bananas, brugmansias (or angel's trumpets) and a host of unusual plants, such as pink sugar cane, have found their place.

Plants are from areas with a similar latitude—northern Vietnam, southern China and Japan, India, southern Africa, South America and our own eastern seaboard. The southern states of the United States on the Atlantic seaboard (Louisiana, Georgia, Florida and Texas) also have similar conditions.

Design Elements

Theme The theme is subtropical, with plants chosen for their ability to make a good fit with the prevailing climatic conditions. They thrive with minimal attention and minimal irrigation, growing well mostly on natural rainfall, which, apart from occasional dry spells, is usually high.

Space The block is long and narrow but the dense planting makes it seem much wider. The deck area is partially enclosed with an encompassing vine, herald's trumpet (*Beaumontia grandiflora*). This beauty flowers in winter when tropical gardens in cooler areas can be a bit plain and devoid of blooms. Partial enclosure tunnels the view, focusing attention to a narrow space. Here, a narrow pathway lined with a complex mix of foliage and flowers creates the illusion of space. The eye darts from side to side and from feature to feature to take it all in. The resulting impression is of a garden that is much bigger.

Texture is important in this garden. Planting thickly makes the plants appear as a block even though the foliage is a mix of strap-leafed, small and large leaves with squat bush forms and erect plants. When we look along the view they register as a unified tapestry rather than individual plants.

At a Glance

Complexity Plant-rich but not difficult

Ability Experienced plantsperson

Maintenance Moderate

The natural advantages of this site, together with careful positioning of the backbone plantings, have created conditions that allow this variety of foliage types to thrive here, giving this lush ambiance.

Colour Close to the house, the deck is the main viewing position and colourful standout plants are grouped around this section. There is an abundance of red-flowered and pink-foliaged plants in this section. Among them are *Costus comosus* syn. *C. barbatus*, *Ruellia elegans*, *Scadoxus multiflorus* var. *katherinae* and a red-leafed *Canna* x *generalis*. Grouping them close to the viewpoint foreshortens the view, making the distance seem further away.

Plants

Some surprising introductions from subtropical nurseries include Philippines coral and pink beauty *Medinilla magnifica*, Siam tulip gingers (*Curcuma alismatifolia*) and a few parrot beaks or crab claws, members of the heliconia family.

Abyssinian banana (*Ensete ventricosum*) is a short-lived giant. It grows quickly, blooms, and like all bananas, dies, within the space of a few years. It's great for instant impact, shade, a strong vertical accent and attractive foliage. The clumping blood banana (*Musa zebrina*) produces new stems each year.

Spiral ginger (*Costus barbatus*) is a novelty. Most costus are true tropicals and resent our cooler winter—but not this one. It grows to over 2 metres and produces brilliant sulphur yellow flowers inside burgundy bracts around Christmas, lasting until autumn.

Begonia 'Golden Girl' has large, shiny lime green leaves. Contrast it with other foliage plants such as vibrant crimson and burgundy bloodleaf (*Iresine herbstii*) or blackish purple *Alternanthera dentata* 'Purple Splash'. The latter two are extremely versatile: use them as spot colour, an informal low shrub or formal hedging.

It's big, it's vigorous and it's fragrant—Burmese honeysuckle (*Lonicera hildebrandiana*), the largest of the honeysuckles, needs a strong support. Trained on stainless steel wires, it forms a semi-formal frame to one side of the garden. Prune it regularly or it can take over a small area.

Variegated sugar cane (*Saccharum officinarum variegata* 'Jamaican Grass') has stripes of pink, purple and bronze. A naturally occurring sport, it once had a practical role as a marker for rows of trial sugar cane. It came from a north coast nursery. Unlike ornamental grasses used in drier southern gardens, it stands up to humid conditions, adding height and a snappy, strappy contrast to the border.

If you can't live without a rose, try *Rosa chinensis* from tropical Asia. 'Mutabilis' and 'Comptesse du Caÿla' are found in heritage rose nurseries. Others like the Vietnamese rose, the recently introduced 'One Thousand Lights' and *Rosa sanguinea* 'Miss Lowe's Rose' are still in the development stages and should be released soon.

Above: *Grewia occidentalis* or lavender star flower is a South African plant that grows in coastal, mountain and grassland sites. It is a frost-tender shrub for full-sun positions.

Opposite: Layering of plants such as cannas, dianella and painted banana creates an interesting tapestry effect, even when flowers are few.

A Succulent Courtyard

This narrow front garden has a distinct South American feel, with its enclosed courtyard and solid timber gate. Bright white walls face north so it is exposed to maximum sun, perfect for succulents and other dry-adapted plants—the perfect solution for owners who did not have time to garden but loved plants.

The space has a lot in common with small townhouse developments, with paving and rendered walls reflecting a lot of light and heat. Under the eaves the ground stays dry, which makes this a good location for succulents.

Low-maintenance Succulents

The owners are often away on business and needed a diverse, low-maintenance garden. Succulents are ideal for busy people and seem to prefer minimal attention. Water or feed them too much and they become soft and sometimes rot at the base or suffer from fungus attack, especially in humid, summer conditions.

Too Humid for Succulents?

Succulents need a dry atmosphere and resent humid conditions, yet this garden is located in a suburb on Sydney Harbour that has high rainfall and humid summers. However, the paved surface reduces humidity around the stems and planting in pots and raised beds gives the plants sharp drainage. In a humid climate, standard soil or potting mixes may become too wet in summer. Many premium mixes sold for terracotta and clay pots include additional water-saving gels or crystals to help plants cope with southern and inland summer dry periods. In a humid, wet summer environment these swell up and allow moisture to sit around the roots of moisture-susceptible plants. Use a coarse, fast-draining potting mix.

Succulents need occasional water in dry and hot summer periods but mostly they cope with only natural rainfall. In a drought they should be watered, for despite the popular notion that these desert plants thrive in Death Valley conditions, all succulents love moisture—just not too much. In the wild, they benefit from night-time dew and often cold temperatures.

Plants

Euphorbia trigona has three-sided stems. It is often multi-branched and the stems exude a milky sap that can irritate skin. It prefers frost-free conditions.

Agave attenuata is the most common of the agaves and its stems are quite soft and spineless, unlike its relatives. It grows in garden beds provided it has good drainage.

Design Elements

Structure White stucco walls are a great foil for architectural plants such as cactus and tall upright succulents such as crassula, euphorbia, yucca and agave. Silhouettes of their strong angular shapes stand out against the walls.

Space The space is quite narrow and is used as an entrance-way as well as a passage to the rear garden. Container plantings can be moved and mostly they occupy the area near the wall so they do not block the narrow passageway. Clustering pots of lower growing plants contributes to the fullness of the planting even though there is plenty of ground space left and a strong sense of openness.

Colour Cactus and succulents flower prolifically in season, often with quite flamboyant and beautiful blooms. However, for most of the year they are quiet and subdued, the foliage textures carrying the garden. The main splash of colour is the crimson bougainvillea. Many of the succulents have subdued leaf colours that contribute to the overall scheme but don't compete with the bougainvillea.

Support Bougainvillea is a vigorous climber and needs a strong frame for support. The large beams of the pergola are stained so they don't need to be repainted. If building one, make sure it is high enough for both passage underneath and the trailing branches of the vine. Bougainvillea's vicious spines are adapted flower buds. If the plant is pruned, overfed and overwatered, it converts them to spines to support the new water shoots that develop, or to reattach itself to a support. Reducing water is one way to ensure they form flowers.

With a largely succulent planting scheme, the garden is a symphony of sharps. The bougainvillea, draped from a strong pergola, is 'Mrs Butt', an old variety but no less useful for that.

At a Glance	
Complexity Low	
Ability General gardener	
Maintenance Moderate	

A Woodland Garden

Many suburban gardens have large and established trees that cast shade over part or most of the garden. As housing densities increase, and bigger houses occupy smaller blocks, shade can be an important decider of garden style.

This is the long, narrow garden of a semi-detached house. Tall trees and dense underplanting create a cool, woodland effect. Overall, the garden borrows much from Japanese design principles and this was a direct result of the owner's interest in bonsai earlier in her gardening career. The dominant colour is green; foliage is the main attraction.

Resolving the Paving

The back had been completely paved with bricks and used as a garaging space for cars when the new owner first arrived. Ripping up the bricks was one option, but there were also large trees including a mature jacaranda, which cast dense shade and have competitive roots. Rather than removing bricks to create a central lawn, a rockery-style planting was adopted. Removing some pavers from the edges created planting pockets for larger trees and shrubs. Planting soil was built up around a curving rock edge and piled over the pavers. This created a shallow but effective planting space which tree roots could not penetrate. The trees were undisturbed and low shrubs and soft perennials thrive.

Heavy Shadows

Overhanging trees made the space seem dark. A golden locust (*Robinia pseudoacacia* 'Frisia') at the end of the garden brightens the long view and its light colour is a good foil to the darker greens around. On the ground, light foliage tonings were added, with silver flashes of dead nettle (*Lamium maculata*). Look for varieties 'Beacon Silver' and 'White Nancy'. White flowers also brighten the gloom. Chinese star jasmine flowers most of the summer, with the main flush in November. Saxifrage or mother of millions (*Saxifraga stolonifera*) has delicate panicles of white flowers and spreads by runners. Tree begonias and gardenias add white flowers in summer, and in sunnier spots, pelargoniums.

Creating Privacy

The garden is quite narrow and the boundaries were prominent. Privacy was an issue as adjacent houses overlooked the space. The boundaries were thickly planted, completely hiding the side fences and disguising the narrowness. With neighbours hidden, all that is seen is the borrowed landscape view of the trees, which gives an illusion of width. The eye is directed upwards and away from the limiting side barriers.

A combination of large trees and overplanting help make the back garden seem much larger than it is. Filling an area, while still leaving open space, tricks the eye into seeing it as larger.

Far left: The entrance to the front door is through a garden of shrubs of varying sizes and spreads. The wall on the left is festooned with flowing Chinese star jasmine, a complement in fragrance to the *Gardenia* 'Magnifica' flowering in November. On the opposite side, a large nandina hides the neighbouring house from view.

Top left: The front garden is a small square space but the meandering path 'lengthens' the route travelled, creating turns that invite examination.

Top right: In the back garden, attention is drawn to small vignettes such as this mirror fronted by candlesticks. Establishing a series of focal points that blend in with the overall theme helps the eye to linger and the brain to 'enlarge' the space.

Bottom: Even the table appears more generously proportioned than it is because it is set into a niche in the paving.

Plants

The following plants have light-coloured foliage suitable for woodland effects.

Trees

Acer negundo 'Elegans'—pale green leaves edged yellow

Acer platanoides 'Drummondii'; 'Norway Maple'—leaves margined creamy white

Shrubs

Arundinaria variegata—dark green leaves striped creamy white

Aucuba japonica 'Picturata'—golden centre, deep green margin

Cornus alba 'Elegantissima'—pale green with silver variegations

Elaeagnus x *ebbingei* 'Gilt Edge'—leaves margined with gold

Euonymus 'Silver Queen'—creamy white and cream variegated

Osmanthus heterophyllus 'Variegatus'—leaves edged creamy white

Phormium 'Tricolor'—bright green leaves striped white and red

Phormium cookianum 'Cream Delight'—green and cream 'swords'

Phormium 'Variegatum'—leaves striped creamy yellow and green

Pieris japonica 'Variegata'—leaves variegated creamy white

Silver foliage

Cushion bush (*Leucophyta brownii*)

Dichondra 'Silver Dollar'—groundcover for dryish spots

Euphorbia characias ssp. *wulfenii*; honey flower (*Melianthus major*)—blue–grey subshrub

Plectranthus argentatus

Yucca species

Cream foliage

Hibiscus 'Roseflake'—attractive pink and cream foliage, red flowers; subtropical, prefers some shade

Pisonia umbrellifera—New Zealand plant with cream and white leaves

Lime green foliage plants

Begonia 'Baby Doll'

Light-coloured flowers for dark corners

White-flowered honesty (*Lunaria annua* 'Variegata')

Pittosporum 'James Stirling'

At a Glance	
Complexity	Low
Ability	General gardener
Maintenance	Moderate

Going Troppo

Tropical style is big throughout the world, from the frosty Northern Hemisphere to our home shores. Along the east coast, and even in temperate Melbourne, it is possible to have a garden that looks 'tropical' by using large-leafed plants from temperate regions.

These three gardens show different ways to get the look in different locations and the problems each garden faces. One is an inner city terrace, and two are suburban gardens. One is located in Sydney's western suburbs where winters are regularly frosty and birdbaths freeze over.

Garden 1: A Collector's Garden

This tropical-style garden in Sydney's western suburbs survives against the odds. Frosty winters would kill such a garden normally but the owner used plants to create a microclimate to protect her cordyline collection.

The theme was determined by the tropical nature of the plant collection. The owner expanded her collection of other subtropical plants such as palms and bromeliads so the cordylines would fit comfortably in the garden. A large pool house designed like a tropical Asian pavilion protects plants on the edge of the garden. Bromeliads and other epiphytic plants grow under the protection of the roof, while cordylines form an outside wall. The bromeliad collection sits in a rockery around the pool.

A Tropical Garden in a Non-tropical Climate

The garden is located in a district where summers are hot and winters frequently drop below zero: establishing a tropical garden in this climate was a tough ask. The old garden was a mix of cooler climate shrubs and trees, many deciduous, which did not really live up to the summer conditions and looked rather forlorn in winter.

The planting has created a microclimate that protects the tropical plants. Wind barriers shield tender specimens from hot summer westerly winds and cold winter southerlies. Taller palms and large shrubs trap warm air in winter to prevent soil cooling. Running water from ponds prevents the water freezing in winter and helps maintain a warm ambient temperature.

An Organic Garden

The owner is a horticulturist and wanted to grow organically, avoiding the use of chemicals and insecticides. Ponds dotted around the garden harbour native animals including several uncommon species of frog, which are happy to enjoy the protection afforded by the cordylines. They hide by day in the folds of the leaves and feed on small snails, insects and other pests, ensuring the garden is relatively free of common garden nasties. They seem happy to live among the bromeliads suspended in hanging baskets, too. Lizards, particularly blue tongues, clean up any adult snails so the cordylines are free of snail or slug damage.

Overplanting and establishing a contrast between dark and light makes this narrow passage seem quite generous. It is set within an average-sized garden.

At a Glance

Complexity Moderate

Ability Advanced gardener

Maintenance Moderate

Garden 2: Inner City Jungle

City living can be very un-private, especially when a large block of flats goes up on your boundary. This is the problem faced by the owner of this semi-detached house in the inner city. After planting, the overall effect is that of a small tropical glade filled with the scent of frangipani and colourful foliage.

Creating Privacy

Privacy was the main problem. The apartment building over-looking the backyard was three storeys tall. Neighbouring trees such as a large golden rain tree (*Koelreuteria paniculata*) gave some cover but were supplemented by palms and other narrow trees that would not spread too far over the garden. Several clumps of golden cane palms (*Dypsis lutescens* syn. *Chrysalidocarpus lutescens*) offer lower storey cover; taller foxtail palms (*Wodetia bifurcata*) hide the upper storeys.

An Outdoor Living Area

The owner wanted to use the garden as an entertaining and relaxation area. Once the privacy planting was sorted, the centre section was paved with sandstone and a wooden deck at the end of the house provides all-weather cover for the dining table and seating. The surrounding beds are filled with a mix of foliage plants including pink banana (*Musa velutina*), elephant's ear (*Alocasia macrorrhiza*), *Ctenanthe* 'Silver Star', *C. lubbersiana* and *C. oppenheimiana* 'Tricolor'.

Above: This subtropical profusion helps block the view of the apartment block behind this semi-detached Victorian home. The garden has a warm, embracing sense of enclosure, as if suddenly alighting at a jungle clearing. Big leaves and the clumping of plants helps achieve this result.

Garden 3: Suburban Subtropical Style

This garden is on a small block that was part of a 1970s subdivision in hardcore suburbia. In spite of the suburban surroundings, and the potential for frost, the owner wanted a rainforest retreat and an interesting outlook from the house.

Creating Privacy

Privacy was a major consideration as neighbours overlooked the garden on three sides. The owner planted a belt of tropical plants in a wide bed. Many are native shrubs and trees, including palms and lilly-pillies. These have grown to form a screen that protects the occupants from prying eyes and blocks out the view of neighbouring houses. All that is seen are the neighbourss trees, part of the borrowed scenery.

Making the Garden Look Bigger

The owner wanted to make this small garden appear larger. Although the garden bed has been made generally wide, in some parts it narrows so there appear to be little alcoves or paths drifting off into the distance. Some paths are included within the beds themselves so the viewer can stroll around and find hidden corners. Shaded alcoves and arbours under trees and vines create cool spots to sit in summer and warm nooks in winter. All these techniques help create the illusion of more space. Additionally, both the funnelling of views of the garden through branches and openings, and the winding areas of lawn, accentuate the illusion.

Getting the Tropical Look

Mixing foliage textures gives the garden a natural look. Where a more cultivated appearance is needed, such as along the path from the back door, mass planting techniques are used. Gingers and scented spider lilies are a bold foreground planting to the forested look behind.

Delicate plants are protected from cold by first establishing a canopy of foliage in case of winter frost. This provides shelter and a blanket of warm air that prevents frost from settling. It also keeps the garden warm in winter.

Below: Layers of planting are repeated here, first with the formal mondo grass edging, then with groups of plants and foliage textures.

A Blended Garden

A combination of plants from many lands can create an eclectic hybrid garden style. This small courtyard uses a core planting of Australian plants blended with succulents from South Africa and the Americas, architectural plants originating in New Zealand and the odd southern African protea. In a broad sense all have a Gondwanan origin and work particularly well together.

Southern Hemisphere plants also seem to share some interesting characteristics. Sometimes it is an ability to withstand hot dry conditions and periodic drought. Other times it is an adaptation to infertile soils, phosphorous intolerance or a similarity of foliage and growth habit. All things considered there is no reason why native plants cannot be integrated into a broader garden composition.

A water feature in the garden is made from Moroccan-style tiles. Aligned with the back door, it forms the main focal point for the garden. On either side stand two large *Yucca elephantipes* in a formal rendition. These two keep the formal axis strong, but beyond this central planting the species composition changes. A blend of exotic and native species forms a tapestry effect. Boldly coloured flowers vie with foliage colour, shape and texture to create a garden that is like a Persian carpet.

Above: *Crassula falcata* has striking orange–red flowers in late summer to autumn.

Right: A blend of exotics, including succulents, palms and grasses are interplanted with native hardenbergia and kangaroo paws to create a unique effect.

At a Glance

Complexity Moderate

Ability General gardener

Maintenance Low

By carefully matching the water and soil needs of the plants, Australian natives and exotics can be grown safely together.

How to Successfully Mix Natives and Exotics

The idea of mixing natives and exotics is all very well but how do you go about it? Here, the native species were treated as the star performers and backbone planting instead of bit players. While they were growing, exotics and short-term native perennials filled the void and provided floral interest. Principal among the natives are kangaroo paws in the 'Bush Gem' series and Sydney flannel flowers (*Actinotus helianthi*). Plants were chosen to suit the climatic conditions. Consider the integral qualities of the plants, such as leaf shape and texture, flower colour, habit and requirements, and choose those that will work well together.

Outdoor Living Space

The owner uses the garden for large-scale family get-togethers and wanted a large open space for sitting and dining. Here, a well-planted perimeter garden surrounds an open area paved with slate that is easy to sweep and keep clean.

The beds are narrow but they are packed with interesting plants that blend together as one. The perimeter planting works as a stroll garden, a place to wander and drink in the beauty of the plants. The tapestry effect of the succulents, kangaroo paws and flannel flowers has a dominant visual impact but the garden will evolve as the background planting matures.

A Square Garden

This small garden at the rear of a semi-detached house is a haven in the inner city. It is made exciting by the use of plant textures and a strong linear design, achieving a strong sense of balance.

A square-shaped garden can be difficult to get right—it can look squat and flat. However, design illusions can both disguise and make the most of the limitations. This is a plant-lover's garden but it is also used extensively for entertaining and relaxation. The timber deck is a practical and inexpensive way to create a sense of openness within plant-rich surroundings.

A square shape can be made to seem wider by using lines that run from side to side—but that can give the impression of lack of depth. Lines from front to rear will give the illusion of greater depth, but at the loss of width.

Making the Most of a Square Shape

The garden is almost square and the surrounding neighbourhood is flat so there is no variation in levels between houses. The solution here was to use line and level changes to alter perceptions of the space. The designer has used latitudinal and longitudinal lines to both broaden and lengthen the square-shaped block. By placing the line of the decking in different directions, with a step up from one to the other, the space appears much bigger. Changing levels gives added depth to the flat site.

At a Glance

Complexity Low

Ability Plant lover's gardener

Maintenance Moderate

A custom-made bench borrows from the shape of a Japanese tori gate, producing seating of amazing grace and elegance. The design, by Peter Vary, is called the Port Fairy chair.

Where to Put Service Areas?

The square shape made it difficult to position service areas. A fenced-off alcove at the rear hides compost bins and the rear lane access. Wheelie bins and other items are completely hidden from view. The intrusion also breaks up the squareness and adds extra spatial dimensions.

Creating Privacy

A trellis at the rear of the property hides neighbouring houses in this densely populated inner-city area, especially while the trees are still growing. A crepe myrtle and a lillypilly hedge will eventually fill out and hide most of the extraneous view at the back. In the meantime, lattice painted to match the fence unifies the whole garden.

Showing off Plants

The transition from one level of decking to another provides different levels for showing off prized plants. The decking allows many plants to be grown in containers, especially a collection of succulents, which may suffer root rot in the open ground. Most need excellent drainage, which was not always possible to guarantee in the clay soil. A raised platform on the right is filled with specimens and gives the garden a lush feel. It also creates a small annex for the custom-made bench. This area, though open from the front, feels secluded when you're sitting there. Without the intrusion of the platform and the dense planting, the garden would be exposed. From the bench, the section to the front and side are partially obscured, adding a sense of mystery and surprise.

Water-savvy planting and containers give the garden a bold edge that combines the best of a minimalist lifestyle with a plant-rich garden. Foliage is the most important part of this planting. Textural contrast is supported by traditional plantings of maple, roses and temperate plants with a tough disposition. The bold dark green leaves of acanthus contrast with the softer greens of Japanese maple (*Acer palmatum*), oakleaf hydrangea (*Hydrangea quercifolia*) and honey bush (*Melianthus major*).

Right: Honey bush (*Melianthus major*) and *Sedum* 'Autumn Joy'

The raised deck, with the planks laid across the block, disguises the squareness of the garden space. Potted plants extend the planting possibilities and hide the shape further.

Finishing
Touches

The finishing touches are often, at least in the long term, among the most important elements of your garden. The preparation and planning is all important but when all is said and done, it is the small details that are visible for years. Our success or failure is judged by them. We remember the finished look not the construction.

Sometimes finishing touches define how we see the garden. Decorative features, the way your plant combinations work and the overall effect often only need a little tweaking to change an ordinary garden into an extraordinary one.

Reflections

Reflections effectively double our perception of any given space. Mirrors are therefore an ideal way to make a small garden look bigger. Used in moderation, mirrors are useful for creating gardening illusions.

Mirrors in a landscape work similarly to the painted trompe l'oeil, creating the illusion of depth. Where the painted effect represents an imaginary or romanticised image, mirrors reflect reality, but in reverse. Several mirrors reflecting each other will create infinite reflections.

Mirrors bring perspective and depth to even the smallest of garden spaces. They need careful positioning as mirrors reflect everything, faults included. If the mirror is positioned in the same way as a bathroom mirror, you will see only your own reflection. In a space where the viewer will step into view constantly, one way to create an illusion of depth without having it destroyed by repeatedly seeing yourself is to disguise the mirror by means of slats. These hide the immediate reflection. Angling the mirror to one side or slightly up or down work similarly.

Take care to ensure that the mirror is not immediately seen as a mirror. The mirror needs to be camouflaged or the illusion is ruined. Mirrors are most effective set within a frame of some sort to disguise their origins. Set within a door or window frame, or recessed within a masonry surround or faux finish, the reflection can seem more convincing, offering a 'view' through a 'glass' panel. Planting around the edges can further disguise the fact that this is an illusion.

Mirrors at ground level are often more convincing at replicating borrowed scenery, but disguise the base so it looks natural and not artificial. Use bricks, gravel or decomposed granite for a seamless finish.

A reflecting ball is one simple way to introduce the illusory effects of mirrors. Most are made of mirrored Perspex, not glass, thus ensuring a longer life. They range in size from about 20 centimetres in diameter to nearly twice that. They generally sit on a plinth or stand or rest among foliage. Along a path or in a garden bed, such a ball reflects its surroundings and gives an illusion of depth. It also attracts attention and heightens the sense of surprise, particularly if discovered just around a corner.

Opposite: A mirror in a tiny garden helps give the illusion of space by reflecting back what is in front of it, but take care with the placement.

Some tweaking is often advisable when installing a garden mirror to make sure it does the job. When fitted on a vertical 90 degree angle the mirror may simply reflect the sky or the neighbour's roof. The aim is to capture a reflection of the garden and make the space appear bigger. Usually the mirror needs to be angled—either up or down—to crop out undesirable views. If a mirror is elevated, say on a retaining wall for instance, you may need to angle it downward so the top captures the view below. With some trial and error, you can get the right angle to maximise the effect. It is not a job for one person; you may need to hire a professional builder or carpenter.

Opposite: A mirror (disguised by a perspective frame) at the end of this patio underneath a deck makes the space seem endless. You would hardly know it is there but it effectively doubles the visual length of the patio.

Below: Using a reflective surface on large glass walls acts exactly like a mirror and 'extends' the perceived view of the garden.

Safety with Mirrors

Alternatives to glass Mirrored perspex is lighter and won't break. It is a useful alternative to glass mirrors but there may be some distortion. Attach the mirror securely to a firm backing board to prevent warping.

Outdoor mirrors Choose mirrors designed for outside use. These are generally of a tougher, thicker glass with a waterproof silver backing. Fix mirrors securely to a wall or fence.

Waterproofing Prevent water getting into the back of the mirror and causing unsightly foxing or spotting by sealing the edges with a silicone sealant such as those used in bathrooms.

Protecting birds Native birds often mistake their own reflection for an intruder and hurl themselves into mirrors to drive them off, especially during the breeding season. Highly territorial birds like wrens or wagtails can sometimes be seriously injured by this behaviour. Place temporary covers over the mirrors and the problem usually goes away.

Children Don't place mirrors where children play, or along well-used passageways where there is a potential for slips and falls, or at the bottom of steps.

Illusions

A favoured trick of renaissance garden design was to paint a view where none existed. The trick is as useful now as it was then.

In a small garden, we need all the help we can get and trompe l'oeil, a French term meaning 'trick the eye', can create an illusion of greater space by creating a 'view' beyond the garden.

The greatest disadvantage of the technique is cost, as it requires artistic skill of a high order. An amateur with some artistic ability could carry it off, but most of us have to rely on professional painters. Trompe l'oeil tends to suit neo-classical or traditional styles of garden, since most practitioners seem to prefer pastoral nostalgic and romantic revival scenes. There is no reason, however, why a contemporary or modern minimalist image could not be used.

Trompe l'oeil generally uses a style close to photographic realism (ironically often executed with an almost Victorian romanticism) to convey a three-dimensional impression of a broader landscape. It uses linear perspective to seemingly extend the boundaries of the garden.

Non-painted Illusions

There are ways of tricking the eye that do not involve painting. For instance, fixing a door with frame and lintel onto a wall in an inner-city courtyard can suggest there is a room or a space behind. Adding a mirror with a grilled front can enhance the illusion. The mirror reflects the view behind and the grille, effectively disguising the fact that we are seeing a reverse view. Placement is important here and a potted plant, a shrub or a tree would the best view to reflect. The illusion would be destroyed if only the washing were visible!

In the eighteenth century, 'perspective treillage' was a popular device. It involved fixing decorative trellis to a wall and arranging it to give the impression of receding perspective (see page 202). The usual form is an archway or an arbour. In some cases it is used in conjunction with trompe l'oeil to give a more realistic three-dimensional effect. In such cases, the trellis can be fixed forward of the wall by using wooden plugs. When sunlight hits, a shadow line would appear, making the scene more realistic.

This is a simple perspective illusion of a niche in a wall that appears as a window to a distant landscape. It is not rendered naturalistically but merely suggests a longer perspective. In the longer view of the garden (opposite top), you can see how effectively it serves to expand the available space.

Above: The view of this garden is enlarged by a cherub on the wall in the rear. The cherub is real but the backdrop is not. It is a painted scene, encouraging us to think beyond the square, in this case a painted archway, made realistic by a planting of ivy around it. The illusion is enhanced by repetition of the theme inside the conservatory. The Pompeii-esque peacock on the wall encourages us to perceive the scene both inside and out as an extension of the scene—the whole box and dice in other words. It works. The grandness is carried off with aplomb only because of this audacious trick.

Left: Another trompe l'oeil effect turns a blank wall into a grand, colonnaded building with a view beyond to trees and sky. The immediate planting in front enhances the Mediterranean-style landscape of arched portico. Though close to the wall, the lavender and orange appear to be further away due to the clever juxtaposition of a real brick path and the painted one with its linear perspective. Shadows from the orange tree coming in from the left of the image encourage us to think of this as a three-dimensional image. Keeping a consistency of style is the only way to make this scene realistic. The two terracotta urns in the foreground look like they belong because of the styling.

An Eye for Detail

Gardens that reflect the owner's experience, personality and passions are possibly the most interesting of all. When interests coincide with a planned attention to design principles and artistic expression, the results can be most satisfying. This is one of those gardens.

This garden blends colour themes with the owner's good horticultural knowledge. For instance, microclimates alter the timing of change for deciduous trees so that the colours they produce coincide with flowering times of other plants in the garden. Sometimes this is serendipitous, but a good gardener knows how to exploit these patterns. Art becomes one with the plantings to enhance the garden's green side. Illusions make it appear much bigger than it is. Vistas lead to hidden corners, and surprises appear at each turn for exploring visitors.

This garden is a journey so let's go on a discovery tour to see how to turn principles into finished touches.

Using the illusory effects of mirrors, the gardener has created a still life from pieces of broken mirror and coloured tiles. The mirrored slivers reflect the scene and give extra depth to the garden.

At a Glance

Complexity High
Ability Skilled amateur
Maintenance High

Small, Sloping and Sandy

The garden is quite small, being an average-sized suburban block with a 1960s house. The gently sloping site has a wide side section on one side and a small back garden. The soil is sandy, porous, free draining and lacking in fertility.

The solution to a lack of space was to make every square metre work. Lawn is non-existent. Instead, paths lead you around the garden. Views out, across and even up make the area look bigger. Because there is a lot to see, the tendency is to linger and absorb. It's a good trick: by layering things of interest and making the passage as long as possible, the journey around the garden is lengthened without occasioning any lapse of attention in the viewer.

Design Elements

Space Several spaces on the journey open out and provide places for sitting. Doorways are decorated with tiles to give them greater depth and encourage longer looks.

Theme The garden follows no set theme, which to some represents breaking all the rules. But rules, once we understand them, are made to be broken. It maintains congruity, however, by following design principles. Decorative elements abound and there are borrowings from many cultural garden styles.

Colour Entering the garden from the driveway, the viewer makes a sharp right turn past the house steps lined with a collection of potted succulents into a colour-coordinated garden. The flower colours are largely orange, red and yellow. These are perfect viewed close up, as hot, bright colours tend to foreshorten the view. Each bed is filled with interesting plantings, some with leaf tonings in bronze or purple or variegations.

A garden seat inspired by the park benches of Antonio Gaudi in Barcelona.

Mystery A sense of mystery and surprise permeates the rear garden. The plantings are arranged to lead the viewer along a vista. Here and there, the garden abruptly turns or opens into another section. Narrow, curving, shaded paths invite exploration.

Art Homemade pieces dot the garden, adding further surprises. Taken together, this combination of artistic expression and hidden spaces creates an illusion of space. Mirrors are not simply mirrors in a frame but mirrors cracked or broken then rearranged with precision to imitate the original shape. Mounted on black board, the reflections become abstracted; the effect is to enhance the spatial illusion. Some take on the form of a mirror flower with mosaic tile insets for petals; these reflect seasonal flowers in the garden. The addition of coloured glass and tiles lifts this simple illusion to mosaic art.

Found objects A garden bench modelled on those of Catalan architect Antonio Gaudi sits in one corner. It is decorated with found objects and treasured pieces that had suffered the perils of time. There are plates from Pakistan, old tiles and bottles, a glass stopper from a broken wine decanter and a teapot whose spout had chipped and that once belonged to the owner's grandmother.

Right: A false door decorated with tiles looks inviting, while in front an artful scene is created with cane chairs and an old Chinese umbrella.

Lighting

New types of garden lights have completely transformed how we use the garden at night, as well as changing perceptions of garden aesthetics. The range of lights available nowadays is both extensive and inexpensive so there is no reason not to make the most of them.

Lighting a garden extends our enjoyment of the garden into the evenings, while adding another layer of beauty to our planted spaces.

Once, the main reasons for installing lights in a garden were security and safety—to light paths and steps so we could see where we were going at night. This was especially so if the garden was heavily treed and sloping. Sensor-controlled floodlights helped deter intruders or other uninvited guests (but failed against the infernal early-evening visits of pesky peddlers of religion!) and had a purely functional role. We would light outdoor dining areas for eating, but usually only close to the house where electricity supply was already laid in.

New low-voltage and LED lighting systems have a gentler impact on the garden, with an opportunity to create beautiful, inexpensive and fun effects with light. Nowadays we use lighting for mood and atmosphere as much as security.

There are other design-based reasons to use lighting beyond the purely practical issue of security. The garden at night is one time when mood and function can be placed to the fore. A well-lit garden, and by that I mean one that satisfies the twin needs of practical lighting and mood setting, should lift your spirits. Well-chosen lighting should entice you to sit outside and read a book or relax with friends or family for dinner under the stars.

Lighting creates a sense of intimacy between interior and exterior spaces. Mood-lighting techniques that highlight a featured table, plant or other object, but don't blast either interior or exterior with incandescent light, can blend the internal and external seamlessly at night. This blurring of the boundaries between inside and out is a useful tool for making the small garden seem larger.

Lighting can also introduce a sense of theatre. Coloured lights, whether the traditional carnival type of coloured globe or more contemporary filament lights can bring a touch of whimsy to a night-time scene. Lights secreted in ponds also reflect ripples on walls and plants, adding extra drama.

The careful highlighting of textures and decorative elements, bring a garden to life. Uplights bring out hidden detail or highlight special characteristics of outdoor ornamentation. You could light a favourite tree, piece of garden art or a well-loved plant.

Above: Light reflected up lines in a sheet of frosted glass changes by means of a transformer fitted behind the bench.

Opposite: Fibre optic lighting comes in 'strings' that can be wound up trunks as with these black bamboo stems. Colours change every few seconds, creating a fascinating light show.

Hanging light globes are an interesting diversion from standard bulbs.

A close-up shows how fibre optics produce an ethereal lighting effect.

Types of Lighting

Put simply, there are two broad categories of external lighting: ornamental and hidden. Ornamental lights become part of the structure of the garden and are generally on show day and night. Functional fixtures unobtrusively hidden in a wall or under the eaves are useful to light a path or an entrance. In addition, there are three main methods of garden lighting: mains-powered, low-voltage and solar.

Mains It is a legal requirement that a licensed electrician must install outdoor power sources using the main electricity supply. This makes it a more expensive operation as trenching and backfilling can be a major part of the cost. Doing this part of the job yourself will save you money but check before digging to make sure of the proper location of trenches. Cabling needs to be encased in conduit and buried a specified depth in the ground. Outdoor mains lighting needs a switching unit independent of your domestic supply and it is a good idea to ensure your electrician adds a safety trip meter to cut supply in case of damage.

Low-voltage lighting also connects to the mains supply but it is converted to 12 volts via a transformer. The transformer simply plugs into an outside socket or a source that is usually kept under cover. Low-voltage cables from the transformer deliver the power to the light units. The major disadvantage of this system is that lights further from the supply often appear dimmer and most transformers available will only provide enough power for a limited number of lights. Transformer outputs vary so consider buying one with the highest load. The alternative is to use many different transformers for each lighting job.

Solar power is the most energy-efficient light source. The problem until now has been that most systems have not provided enough light when it is most needed. Solar lights store the sun's energy during daylight hours and begin illuminating at dusk. For paths this is fine, but solar lights tend to dim after a few hours of use. They are improving, with more expensive solar lights lasting for up to 12 hours. Solar lights often give a cold blue cast to the garden, which is not particularly attractive. Use them by all means, but their colour and intensity make them best suited to lighting paths and other functional purposes. Solar lights have one other disadvantage— they are easy to steal. The lighting posts can be lifted out of the ground as there is no wiring attaching them to other fittings. They are one of the most commonly stolen items from unsecured front gardens.

Light emitting diodes (LED) are a high-tech form of lighting used in computers and other high-end consumerables. LED lights are long lasting and environmentally sound. Unlike traditional lights, LEDs do not have a bulb and hence have no filament to blow. Instead electrons produce the light. Diodes don't wear out like bulbs either, giving a diode a life of 30 000–50 000 hours. As they last for many years, the unit is effectively sealed for life. They use less power than low-voltage halogens but a single diode emits only a small amount of light, so each light consists of a cluster of diodes. LEDs use minute quantities of low-voltage electricity and are much cheaper to run than other lights. Unlike halogen, the diodes do not get hot and won't burn, so they are safer around children. They also do not attract insects. Lights are available in a range of colours. These are only visible when the light is switched on.

On the downside, apart from the coloured lights, the 'white' lights can have a cold bluish cast compared to the yellow–white spectrum of halogen and many are needed to effectively illuminate a large area. For paths, or for mood and effect, they are ideal. Individual units still cost more than halogen (as does solar) but running costs and maintenance are far lower. LEDs need to be connected to a transformer.

A custom-made water feature for a small apartment balcony is made from strips of coloured perspex panels. It combines the magical effect of moving water with a space-age light show. Water flows over the top and down the sides; the light catches it, throwing shimmering reflections onto the walls. *Mandevilla* x *amoena* 'Alice du Pont' grows up a wire frame on the wall.

Less is better The key to good garden lighting is restraint. Aim for a subdued light that accents features and does not overwhelm.

Feature the garden, not the lighting Accentuate the features of the garden and make it safe to traverse; don't turn night into day.

Match the lighting to the task Use wall-mounted lights for illuminating an entrance. Choose more appropriate types for feature lighting. Floodlighting may make your pool a safer place to swim at night but it makes plants look washed out.

How wide do you want to cast light? For a wide field of light with downlights, place the fitting higher. Fittings lower to the ground will cast a more pin-like light. For a path, you can light only the path or the borders on either side as well.

Plan for future expansion Buy a bigger transformer than you currently need and to leave scope for adding extra wire when the lights are hooked up.

Plan ahead for your switching control needs Switching on lighting can be a pain if you have to walk a long distance. Plan your switching devices for convenience. They range from manual wall systems to daylight sensors and remote control systems with dimmers.

Highlight focal points Uplights and downlights are particularly effective to highlight distant objects or plants at night.

Consider your neighbours Light pollution from sensor lights or from badly directed floods and uplights could annoy neighbours. Check that your lights are not directed into neighbours' property.

Plan lighting for effect If you have different lighting needs, such as path lighting and mood lighting, put them on different circuits. They can cancel each other out if used together.

Coloured filters Use these with discretion. They can cause plants to look unnatural. However, they have their uses. A blue filter on an underwater light or near a pond can bring the water to life at night.

Subdued uplighting show off a series of container-grown yuccas, offering a sophisticated effect visible from the living room to the right of the picture.

Lighting Techniques

Spotlights are most often used to highlight large architectural features, garden statues and special trees, creating dramatic effects and drawing the eye towards the lit object. They work well when viewed from a reasonable distance.

Uplights light upright objects, such as the crown of a tree or large shrub, from beneath, casting a peripheral glow on surrounding areas. Set lights at ground level so they point up to light the branches against the night sky or dark background. This technique will help add height to a city garden. Face lights away from the viewing point to avoid seeing the glare from the bulb.

Downlights reveal textures and highlight specific objects. Downlighting focuses light into a tree or onto a ground space from above. Lights can be mounted on a wall or in a tree. A series of lights set into the branches of a tree imitates the moonlight and outlines the shape of the tree or casts interesting branch patterns on surfaces. Use downlights to create pools of light for visual impact or for subtle functional uses, such as marking the passage through an arbour.

Skimming is a soft lighting technique for lighting walls and hard landscaping structures. Place lights at an angle to highlight textures, such as the surface of bricks, slats of a fence or the undulations in a slate path. Night lighting tends to deaden flower colour, but skimming light over a painted wall can bring colour into the night garden. It highlights the layout and structure of a garden at night.

Submerged lighting can create a variety of night-time effects and alert visitors about a potential danger. Underwater lighting gives a glow to the surface of a water feature and the ripples are seen as moving patterns on reflected surfaces. Placing waterproof lights in ponds is especially effective where water cascades. A waterfall can be turned into a cascade of light with effective lighting.

Silhouetting creates a theatrical shadow on a wall. Light a plant or sculpture from the front to cast a shadow that varies according to the distance of the light from the object. Hide the light fitting for maximum effect.

Wall-mounted lights are usually placed at eye level. Use translucent panels such as frosted or sandblasted glass to ensure a wash of diffused light.

Fibre optic lighting is a relatively new form of lighting in gardens. It allows creative, even theatrical, effects with low energy consumption. As the name implies, it uses an optical panel to distribute light through a series of bundled fibres—usually plastic or glass. It produces a low ambient light used for outlining hard landscaping elements, and end-emitting systems for tying onto living plants or directing onto glass panels. The changing colours, glowing and twinkle effects are much more sophisticated than older bud light systems.

Bollard lights are low-standing lights (up to 1 metre high) with a light on top. They are useful for lighting pathways or entries.

Pole tops are about 2.5 metres tall. They are used mainly for lighting paths and driveways. Styles range from traditional coach lights to modern, plain spheres.

Non-electric alternatives include garden flares, candles in Chinese or Japanese stone lanterns, or groupings of candles.

Top: This glowing glass block is a subtle lighting effect suitable for an intimate courtyard.

Bottom: This sculptural water feature offers subtle lighting effects combined with recessed uplights set into the decking.

Topiary

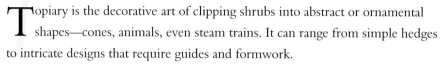

Topiary is the decorative art of clipping shrubs into abstract or ornamental shapes—cones, animals, even steam trains. It can range from simple hedges to intricate designs that require guides and formwork.

This ancient art introduces a three-dimensional effect in a small garden. Generally used in classical or formal gardens, with a bit of tweaking topiary also works in a modern or minimalist garden.

True topiary takes years to grow and train, but for a quicker effect try some shortcuts, for example training fast-growing climbers such as ivy or muehlenbeckia onto wire frames.

What Plants Should I Use?

Use evergreen plants, preferably with fine foliage. Conifers and small-leaf privet (make sure all flowers are removed and choose one of the less invasive ones like *Ligustrum longifolia*) were traditionally used but popular modern plants are box, rosemary, westringia, diosma, melaleuca, pittosporum, figs (*Ficus hillii* and *F. benjamina*), camellia, lonicera and lillypilly. Species should have small leaves, thick growth and be fast growing so that clipping wounds repair promptly.

To train into shapes (rather than just clipping) choose ones with long, flexible stems that can be bent, tied or wired.

Chinese star jasmine (*Trachelospermum jasminoides*) is a versatile climber that can be used as a shrub, groundcover or, as here, a topiarised hedge. It grows fast and needs regular attention to get it to look as manicured as this. Its main blooming time is November but some scented flowers appear throughout the warmer months.

Get the Most from Your Topiary

- Keep your design simple to minimise maintenance; new growth can quickly obscure the shape of complicated patterns.
- Easy shapes to maintain are pyramids, balls, cones and 'poodle cut'.
- Clip new shoots regularly to prevent leggy growth and maintain the desired form.
- Feed with a good slow-release fertiliser.
- Protect plants from strong winds. Standards are especially prone to damage.
- Water regularly and do not allow soil to dry out. Moisten leaves after pruning.
- Repot in the main growing season—early to mid spring is best. Repotting into a larger container allows standards to develop a larger ball and a thicker, more imposing trunk.
- Don't squeeze plants into corners; where possible turn them fortnightly to ensure each side receives adequate sunlight.

How Do I Start Topiary?

Decide on the style you want. A simple geometric shape is easiest for the beginner. Start with a thin single-stemmed plant and remove all lower leaves and branches. A standard design needs to be staked to keep the trunk straight. Careful pruning over the growing season encourages more new shoots and a denser habit. Prune regularly throughout the life of the plant whether it is grown in a container or in the ground.

How Can I Use Topiary in My Landscape?

Topiary can fit into traditional or modern garden styles. If you can afford ready-made plants, this is the nearest thing yet to an instant garden for courtyards, balconies or townhouses. Ready-made standards, balls and cones are available from garden centres. Arrange them as if they were pieces of garden sculpture.

A topiarised ball can be a charming table feature. Try small-leafed box or honeysuckle (*Lonicera nitida*).

Conifers of various types make interesting topiary effects. The classic one is yew but it needs a cooler climate than that afforded by most of Australia. Instead consider book-leaf thuja (*Thuja occidentalis*), *Juniperus virginiana* 'Spartan', Bhutan cypress (*Cupressus torulosa*) and Hollywood juniper (*Juniperus chinensis* 'Kaizuka').

Espalier

In a small space, it's often necessary to use every surface to the max. Espalier enables us to use the vertical space of walls in a way that is both practical and aesthetic.

An espaliered plant is one that has been trained to grow two-dimensionally on a flat plane. In the seventeenth century, 'espalier' referred to the frame or trellis on which the plant was trained but today it refers to both the plant and training technique.

The technique stems from ancient times. The city gardens of Rome were enclosed by walls and were often as small as those of our modern townhouses. Gardeners learned that they could produce a crop of fruit by training trees into two-dimensional shapes along sunny walls.

Espalier is well suited to contemporary gardens, especially those in city locations where walls and small space preclude growing trees that would otherwise overwhelm the garden area. Espalier can also be used in conjunction with trompe l'oeil and other false perspective devices to create an illusion of receding distance. By reducing the space between the wires as they recede towards the back of a small property, we can present a false perspective.

Today, espaliered trees, both ornamental and fruit producing, can be grown against walls as well as free-standing on wires.

Above: Apples are often grown as espalier or on a wire framework. It enables them to be grown in a confined space and, especially in cooler climates, growing on a wall aids ripening of the fruit. Specialist fruit growers often have partly trained trees for sale but it pays to read as much as you can about pruning and training apples to ensure maximum fruit production.

Right: One of the easiest plants to grow in an espalier form is Chinese star jasmine, here growing on diamond-patterned stainless-steel wires stretched over the wall. As well as being an artistic way of growing this plant, it also offers textural quality.

How to Espalier a Tree in a Small Space

Taut wires tied between posts are usually used but lattice provides an easy frame. Sun-loving plants like oleander should face north for maximum sun exposure.

Choose healthy one- or two-year-old plants with supple branches that already correspond to the eventual shape. Remove any forward-facing branches and any that do not conform to the plane. Secure retained branches to the frame with plastic budding tape or other soft bindings. Pinch back where necessary so the plant conforms to your final plan.

Types of Espalier

Cordon or horizontal cordon Allow the central leader to grow three pairs of horizontal shoots either opposite each other or alternately, depending on the growth habit. Equal spacing between each tier makes it more appealing. The first year, prune the newly planted sapling early in spring to the desired height of the first tier, usually about 30–45 centimetres above the ground. Progress in subsequent years selecting the number of tiers you can reasonably attend to.

Palmette verrier This is a variation on the basic horizontal cordon. Train lateral shoots horizontally at first and then direct them upwards to form a candelabra-like shape. This is also sometimes referred to as U-shaped.

Fan Train branches upwards from a single point near the base and allow them to form an outward fan shape.

A complex and labour-intensive form of espalier is this multiple cordon. The plant used is pyracantha and there are several different forms. However, their potential for being dispersed by birds into bushland has made them one of the prime suspects for the weed vigilantes.

The Mosaic Garden

Imagine a small bejewelled box inlaid with glistening gems that glow like gold or silver. Then imagine this same jewellery box writ large. Now you can appreciate the intricacy and work that makes a mosaic garden so precious.

Melbourne's mosaic garden is a small self-contained garden hemmed in by a high brick wall, which serves both as canvas and protector. What exists within that wall is an artist's personalised gallery, comprising two linked courtyards behind a converted church hall.

Until the owner's death, it was a work in progress, with mosaics flowing over walls, steps, boulders and containers. Bold architectural plants and mosaics are the main unifying elements. Whimsical gestures add a sense of surprise and the meandering white quartz gravel flooring leads the viewer to mysterious corners made more so by the combination of plants and unexpected colour flourishes.

A garden totally devoted to mosaics is a rarity and this one received international recognition for its innovative and creative approach to the medium. The plantings are fairly simple. The garden is not filled with horticultural treasures, rare or hard-to-grow specimens. Instead, a couple of existing camphor laurels (*Cinnamomum camphora*), a lemon-scented gum (*Corymbia citriodora*), Abyssinian banana (*Ensete ventricosum*), giant bird of paradise (*Strelitzia nicolai*) and a mix of hardy succulents and tough perennials fill the garden with strong upward shapes and foliar structure.

Top: A plinth made from a drain pipe is covered with mosaic tiles and given a new lease of life. Planting should be kept as simple as possible with this high level of decorative treatment.

Bottom: Even the pavers have been mosaic-ed and the effect is quite charming.

Design Elements

Space Sometimes 'less is more' is not the right motto. Sometimes, as here, adding more can make a small space seem larger. The planting is simple, the layout is open and continuous and layering of mosaics ties it together.

Unity The extended mosaic theme holds the garden together. The white quartz gravel on the ground provides a second unifying element. The eye follows the sweeping lines of pattern incorporated in the wall.

Balance Gravel accentuates the light and proffers a neutral backdrop to balance the strong vertical shapes—the upright leaves on many plants, and the decorated plinths, pots and boulders dotted around the space.

Colour The colours the artist used were favourites because they performed particular roles. Turquoise lifts all the other colours and is a great unifier. The apple or acid green is strong on its own but also blends well with everything else. Blue and white are energising and are used lower down in the design, almost like a settling sea. The almost murky, dusky beige pink acts as a

Mosaic has been applied to virtually all surfaces, with attention paid to the colour scheme and the overall effect. Consistency is maintained throughout the work, which took place over many years.

The view into the garden from inside is like looking into a jewel case.

At a Glance

Complexity High

Ability Talented craftsperson

Maintenance Low to moderate

neutralising agent. Blocks of colour form waves that lead the eye around the garden, helping create an illusion of greater space.

Focal points From almost any position the viewer can stand and rotate a full 360 degrees to get a series of different perspectives with new focal points at each turn. As a stroll garden with two distinct courtyards, focal points are important. Fountains are not only seen but also heard. Wall pots, plinths, columns, plant containers and statues are visual focal points.

Theme There are different artistic and cultural influences at play, with the bright colours of Mexico and Santa Fe playing with a selection of dry-climate plants that could be the French Riviera or Southern California. A mosaic table with a billowing tablecloth says Nice or Côte d'Azur.

Mystery and surprise This is a garden where you should expect the unexpected! Curved surfaces and colour changes create illusions of shadow and light as you wander the meandering paths around the mosaic features.

Finish The mosaic tiles are not merely broken tiles or crockery but are carefully cut and assembled, sometimes as a blown out reconstruction of the original, or with glazed features singled out and highlighted.

Plants

Plants were chosen for their ability to blend with the mosaics rather than compete with them. The strong, jewel-like colours in the tiles removed the need for flowers. The owner even cut the flowers from her clivias so they did not clash with the walls and detract from the bold strappy leaves.

A pond is lined with lime green tiles that look like moss. It is surrounded with plants that accentuate the green: Amazon queen (*Alocasia amazonica*) and calla lily (*Zantedeschia aethiopica* var. *childsiana*). On a stepped wall lined with blue and turquoise tiles accented with red and yellow, dwarfed *Aloe arborescens* demand attention. Elsewhere, an old *Agave attenuata* seems to grow organically from the top of a twisted and contorted container so it looks like a triffid turned to stone, or a 'Doctor Who' alien made beautiful by tiled ornamentation. The shapes are also reminiscent of Gaudi's contorted shapes that make Barcelona so famous.

Walls, pots, even rocks are covered with mosaic, creating an attractive art space in a suburban backyard.

Further Reading

Small Gardens

Brookes, John, 1990, *The New Small Garden Book*, Lothian, Melbourne

Durie, Jamie, 2003, *The Outdoor Room*, Allen & Unwin, Sydney

Stevens, David, 2003, *Small Space Gardens*, Conran Octopus, London

Young, Helen, 2005, *Balcony*, Lothian, Melbourn

General Design

Bradley-Hole, Christopher, 1999, *The Minimalist Garden*, Mitchell Beazley, London

Crowe, Sylvia, 1994, *Garden Design*, Garden Art Press, Woodbridge UK

Stevens, David and Buchan, Ursula, 1997, *The Conran Octopus Garden Book*, Conran Octopus, London

Kingsbury, Noel, 2005, *Gardens by Design*, Cameron House, Wingfield, SA

Paul, Anthony, 1994, *Creative Ideas for Small Gardens*, Harper Collins, London

The Sunday Times, 2001, *Small Gardens For Modern Living*, Hamlyn, London

Japanese and Oriental Gardens

Itoh, Teiji, 1973, *Space and Illusion in the Japanese Garden*, Weatherhill/Tankosha, New York

Keswick, Maggie, 2003, *The Chinese Garden*, Frances Lincoln, London

Mizuno, Katsuhiko, 2002, *Landscape for Small Spaces*, Kodansha International, Tokyo

Nitschke, Gunter, 1991, *Japanese Gardens, Taschen*, Cologne

Hayakawa, Masao, 1973, *The Garden Art of Japan*, Art Media Resources, Chicago

Seike, Kiyoshi et al, 1980, *A Japanese Touch For Your Garden*, Kodansha International, Tokyo

South-East Asian and Tropical Gardens

Warren, William, 1995, *Balinese Gardens*, Periplus Editions, Berkeley CA

Wijaya, Made, 2000, *Tropical Garden Design*, Thames & Hudson, London

Native Gardens

Thompson, Paul, 2002, *Australian Planting Design*, Lothian, Melbourne

Urquhart, Paul, 2002, *The New Native Garden*, New Holland Publishers, Sydney

Mediterranean and Dry-climate Gardens

Buendia Julbez, Jose M. et al, 1997, *The Life and Work of Luis Barragan*, Rizzoli NewYork

Goslee Power, Nancy, 1995, *The Gardens of California*, Thames and Hudson, London

Hobhouse, Penelope, 2003, *Gardens of Persia*, Florilegium, Sydney

Jones, Louisa, 1992, *Gardens in Provence*, Flammarion, Paris

Le Blanc, Sydney, 1997, *Secret Gardens of Santa Fe*, Rizzoli New York

Mencos, Eduardo, 2004, *Hidden Gardens of Spain*, Frances Lincoln, London

Credits

Garden Designers

Above the Earth Pty Ltd (NSW) pp. 7, 23
Adam Wright (Vic) pp. 39, 104–5
Amanda Oliver (Vic) pp. 196–97
Andrew Candy (NSW) pp. 184–85
Andrew Davies, ICON (NSW) p. 44l
Andrew O'Sullivan (NSW) pp. 22, 100–103, 110111, 141
Andrew Seccull, Jenny Smith Gardens (Vic) pp. 48, 134–35, 212
Anne Thomson, The Garden Design Studio (NSW) pp. 76–77, 202
Barry Jarrott Arcadian Aspects (NSW) p. 201
Ben Kerr, The Garden Company (Vic) p. 52
Brendan Lewis, Landscapes NSW pp. 50, 192, 193
David Kirkpatrick, Outdoor Creations(VIC) pp. 68–71
David Vago, Habitation (NSW pp. 43t, 208–209, 210tr
Dean Herald, Rolling Stone Landscapes (NSW) pp. 4–5
Fiona Brockhoff and David Swann (Vic) pp. 41, 78–81
Good Manors (NSW) pp. 7, 23
Graham Greenhalgh, Tropic of Sydney (NSW) p. 54
Grant Donaldson, Urban Jungle (NSW) P 47
Gregg Chapman Faulkner & Chapman Landscape Design (VIC) pp.12, 55b, 144–45
Hugh Main, Spirit Level Designs Pty Ltd (NSW) p. 150
Jack Merlo Landscape Design (VIC) p. 35b, 44r, 52r
James Hutchison (VIC) p. 215
Jamie Loft, Out from the Blue (VIC) pp. 15, 166–67, 211
Jim Fogarty Landscapes (Vic) p. 45br, 51br
Joanne Green Landscape Design Pty Ltd (NSW) p. 29
John Shinkfield, PSB/EDAW (NSW) pp. 158–161
Jonathon Garner, Puddleton Cottage Gardens (NSW) pp. 60–63, 216b
Ken Lamb Imperial Gardens (NSW) pp. 25b, 94–95, 142bl
Leaf & Stone (Vic) pp.104–105
Liz McFie & Prue Robertson, Figment Designs (NSW) p. 31b

Made Wijaya (Bali) p. 96
Margaret Cory Garden Designs (NSW) pp. 136–37
Matthew Cantwell Secret Gardens of Sydney Pty Ltd (NSW) pp. 16, 122–25
Michael Bates, Bates Landscape Services Pty Ltd (NSW) p. 53
Michael Cooke, Avant Garden (NSW) p. 33, 40
Myles Baldwin Designer Gardens (NSW) p. 210l
Peter Bachak Osmosis Design (NSW) p. 23
Peter Nixon, Paradisus (NSW) pp. 2–3, 13b, 118, 28, 37, 42, 178–83
Reno Attard (dec'd) pp. 148–149, 156–157
Richard Unsworth Garden Life (NSW) pp. 43b, 46, 56–59
Roni Nettleton, Living Exteriors (VIC) front cover
Ted Smythe (NZ) p. 203
Ted Whitley, Sacred Grove Gardens (NSW) pp. 24, 86–89, 138–39, 194–95
Thomas Ellicott, Concept Green (NSW) pp. 51t, 55r, 97, 130–133
Vladimir Sitta (NSW) pp. 30l, 146–47
Votre Jardin (NSW)p. 90–93

Thanks to the following garden owners:

Amanda Oliver (Vic) pp. 196–97
Andrew O'Sullivan (NSW) pp. 22, 100–103
Ann Gyngell (NSW) pp. 152–53
Anne Meadowes (NSW) p. 95
Anne Pegum (NSW) pp. 50, 193
Anne Thomson (NSW) p. 202
Barry and Gwen McIntosh (Vic) pp. 68–71
Bruce McFee (NSW) pp. 156–57
Dare Jennings (NSW) p. 53
Donna Campbell (NSW) p. 192
Dr Eleanor Hodges (Vic) p. 84–85
Edward Smith & Andrew Treloar (Vic) pp.134–35, 212
Eric Lawrence (NSW) p. 94
Evan Petridis (Vic) pp. 35b, 44r
Fiona Cox (NSW) pp. 82–83
Fiona McGill (NSW) p. 25b
Fred Schiers (NSW) pp. 7, 23
Glenn Callcott (NSW) pp. 118–21
Glenys and Stephen Rowe (NSW) p. 54
Grace Silvio (NSW) pp. 24, 138–139, 194–95

Grant Cameron (NSW) pp. 122–25
Gregg Chapman (Vic) pp. 12, 55b
Helen Curran (NSW) pp. 190–91
Ines and Beat Hutter (NSW) pp. 51t, 130–31
Jamie Loft (VIC) pp.15br, 211
Janette and Bill Narlock (NSW) p. 184–85
Jenny Lane (NSW) pp. 25t, 116, 186–89
Jessica Bowie Wilson (NSW) pp. 150–51
Jill Morrow (NSW) p. 217
Jo Richards (NSW) pp. 110–11, 141
Jo Richards (NSW) pp. 110–111, 141
John Pitt (NSW) p. 20
Judy Cuppaidge (NSW) pp. 17b, 36, 117
Julie Haussmans (NSW) pp. 132–33
Julie Lane (NSW) p. 47
Karen and Paul Murray (NSW) pp. 43b, 46t, 56–59
Karen Middleton (NSW) pp. 28, 38
Kate Moodie and Neil Bowes (NSW) pp. 46b, 60–63
Kath and Peter Edwards (NSW) pp. 15bl, 27b
Lee & Bruce Thomas (NSW) p. 19
Lorna Rose (NSW) pp. 162–165
Margaret Fink (NSW) pp. 30l, 106–109
Margot Knox (VIC) (dec'd) pp. 13t, 218–21
Matt and Sarah Vaughan (Vic) pp. 144–145
Michael Selby and Elena Wise (NSW) pp. 148–49
Nick Jensen and Warren Buchanan (NSW) pp. 114–115
Pam Hawkins (NSW) pp. 128–29
Pamela Polglase (NSW)pp. 31t, 55t, 200, 206–207
Paul Allen and Geoff Jackson (NSW) pp. 35t
Paul Urquhart (NSW) p. 127
Peta Laurison, Grand Illusions (Vic) pp. 204-205
Peter Nixon (NSW) pp.2–3, 13b, 42, 178–183
Rae Bolotin (NSW) pp. 158–161
Ray Hennig (NSW) p.10
Ray Hennig (NSW)p. 10
Roberta Miorelli (NSW) pp. 8–9, 10–11, 98–99
Rosemary Kline (NSW) pp.15t, 72–75
Roslyn & Alex Fischer (NSW) p. 51bl
Sarah Churnside (Vic) p. 48
Stirling Macoboy (NSW) (dec'd) pp. 67
Sue Smith (NSW)pp. 146–47
Sue Wagner (NSW) p. 143
Vanessa Snelling (NSW) pp. 76–77

First published in Australia in 2007 by

Reed New Holland an imprint of New Holland Publishers (Australia) Pty Ltd

Sydney • Auckland • London • Cape Town

1/66 Gibbes St Chatswood NSW 2067 Australia

218 Lake Road Northcote Auckland New Zealand

86 Edgware Road London W2 2EA United Kingdom

80 McKenzie Street Cape Town 8001 South Africa

10 9 8 7 6 5 4 3 2 1

National Library of Australia Cataloguing-in-Publication Data:

Urquhart, Paul, 1952- .

    Small by design: Gardens for any space

    ISBN 9781877069154.

    1. Gardens - Design. 2. Gardens - Planning. I. Title.

    712.6

Publisher: Martin Ford

Project Editor: Yani Silvana

Designers: Greg Lamont, Tania Gomes

Printer: SNP Leefung

Picture credits

Paul Urquhart: pp. 27t, 30r, 66, 96.

Ted Whitley: pp. 86–89

Phil Gray: p. 140

Secret Gardens of Sydney: pp. 122–125